The Sirius: past and present

THE
SIRIUS
PAST AND PRESENT

Graeme Henderson & Myra Stanbury

AUSTRALIA

Australia
1788-1988

This publication was funded by the Australian Bicentennial Authority as part of its National Heritage Program to celebrate Australia's Bicentenary in 1988.

Edited by Margo Lanagan and designed by Steven Dunbar
Typeset in Goudy Old Style by Deblaere Typesetting Pty Ltd
Printed by Mandarin Offset, Hong Kong

COLLINS PUBLISHERS AUSTRALIA
First published in 1988 by William Collins Pty Ltd,
55 Clarence Street, Sydney NSW 2000

Copyright © Text: Graeme Henderson and Myra Stanbury, 1988
© Illustrations: Australian Bicentennial Authority

National Library of Australia
Cataloguing-in-Publication data

Henderson, Graeme, 1947-
 The Sirius.

 Bibliography.
Includes index.
ISBN 0 7322 2447 0.

 1. Sirius (Ship). [2]. First Fleet, 1787-1788.
 3. Convict ships. 4. Shipwrecks – Norfolk
 Island. 5. Underwater archaeology – Norfolk
 Island. I. Stanbury, Myra. II. Title.

910.4'5

All rights reserved. No part of this publication may be reproduced, stored in a retrieval system, or transmitted, in any form, or by any means, electronic, mechanical, photocopying, recording or otherwise, without the prior permission of the publishers.

This book is sold subject to the condition that it shall not, by way of trade or otherwise, be lent, resold, hired out or otherwise circulated without the publisher's prior consent in a form of binding or cover other than that in which it is being imposed on the subsequent purchaser.

Front Cover: The Melancholy Loss of His Majesty's Ship *Sirius,* wreck'd on Norfolk Island, on Friday Noon March 19th 1789 taken from the Flag Staff on the Beach. *Watercolour by George Raper, 1790. By Courtesy of the British Museum (Natural History), London.*

Back Cover: Sirius *Project divers break off chunks of the seabed in Sydney Bay, for laboratory examination by maritime archaeologists. Photograph by Pat Baker, 1987.*
AUSTRALIAN BICENTENNIAL AUTHORITY

Contents

1. New worlds and old freedoms   7
2. Building and outfitting the *Berwick*   36
3. Early voyages   54
4. The commissioning of *HMS Sirius*   59
5. The First Fleet voyage   69
6. A voyage round the world from Port Jackson   74
7. Voyage to disaster   79
8. The archaeology of the *Sirius*   89
9. Relics from the *Sirius*   113
10. Conclusion   146
Glossary   150
References   153
Index   164
Acknowledgments   168

Shoulder-belt plates. Photograph by Pat Baker, 1987.
AUSTRALIAN BICENTENNIAL AUTHORITY

CHAPTER 1
New worlds and old freedoms

'Australia... today stands as a symbol of the New World
and the Old Freedoms...',
Charles Bateson, *The Convict Ships.*[1]

This book traces the short career of a ship that played a minor role in Britain's withdrawal from America and a major role in British expansion into the Pacific. As a Baltic trading ship, the *Berwick* made several voyages to America before being recommissioned as the 20-gun HMS *Sirius*, to escort the First Fleet to Australia in 1787–88. That role accomplished, the *Sirius* assumed the mantle of protector and provider to the infant colony until her loss in 1790 at Norfolk Island.

The remains of the *Sirius* lie in uninviting, turbulent waters off Kingston, Norfolk Island. Maritime archaeologists invited to investigate the shipwreck as an Australian Bicentennial Authority project had little reason to suppose, therefore, that much of the vessel or its contents had survived. Since the commencement of the *Sirius* Project in 1983, however, this early skepticism has been dispelled. Contrary to expectations, archaeological excavation, as this book demonstrates, has produced a substantial quantity of artefacts, many in an excellent state of preservation. These objects now provide a tangible link with HMS *Sirius* and will enable many of the gaps in our knowledge of the vessel to be filled.

The voyage to Botany Bay was the most important event in the history of HMS *Sirius*. Yet her history began some seven years earlier, in 1780. Coincidentally, in July of that year, Arthur Phillip declared, to the First Lord of the Admiralty, his willingness to serve in 'whatever part of the World Service' was offered to him.[2] Little could he know that a vessel then under construction at London's Rotherhithe shipyards would escort him to his post as first governor of New South Wales. Nor that the squadron of ships to accompany him would be carrying a large number of unfortunate British citizens being exiled from their homeland.[3]

By 1780, Britain's sphere of influence encompassed the world. James Cook's voyages of discovery and scientific exploration in the 1770s had brought the final South Pacific frontier within its grasp. However, Britain's prime concerns at this time still lay with Europe, India and the New World colonies. The 'old freedoms' of England still prevailed — political and civil liberties which permitted freedom of speech, thought and social mobility. But new ideas and philosophies, known as the 'Enlightenment' and promoted under the auspices of these freedoms, emphasised social and political inequalities and now threatened Britain's power and control over its North American Empire. Allied to the North American colonists' struggle for independence was Britain's perpetual adversary, France. Spain, the United Provinces and the 'neutral' northern European powers also gave direct and indirect support to the colonists' cause. For the first time, Britain was left to fight a campaign in total diplomatic isolation. The loss of the North American colonies in 1783 undoubtedly undermined Britain's political prestige. There were naturally economic consequences,[4] but contrary to expectations the American War of Independence (1776–1783) did not seriously upset British society, nor did it disrupt the nation's domestic or foreign economy.[5]

British settlement of the east coast of Australia in 1788 is frequently linked with perceived consequences of the war, not the least being Britain's loss of a convenient outlet for its convicts. In this book, however, a wider perspective of Britain's political economy and imperial strategy in the eighteenth century will be presented so that the construction of HMS *Sirius*, her early seafaring history, her suitability as a First Fleet ship, and her role in the colonisation of Australia can be viewed in a broader dimension.

Since the *Sirius* played a crucial part in the founding and early development of the colony, it is pertinent to consider the context of the the British government's decision in 1786 to settle New South Wales. The reasoning for this decision has been the subject of profound debate among Australian historians. Their recent findings shed new light on the event and provide an explanation for the *Sirius'* presence in South Pacific waters at the time of her demise in 1790.

However 'experimental' the colonisation of Australia might have been,[6] the expedition could not have been undertaken without careful preparation. Many historical factors indicate that the venture was not as ill-prepared or haphazardly undertaken as some historians would believe.

THE OLD WORLD AND ITS FREEDOMS

Eighteenth-century Britain was a nation in transition. Its agrarian economy, in which poverty and unemployment were deeply rooted, was giving way to relative prosperity as it emerged as the first industrial nation from 1750 onwards. Underlying Britain's rise to commercial, naval and colonial supremacy in the late eighteenth century was its flexible, coherent social structure, which gave it a degree of internal strength not enjoyed by many of its European neighbours.

Outwardly, the society was 'disparate, fluid, and spangled with contrasts and anomalies'.[7] It was a highly differentiated, complex society unlike that of most European countries.[8] People had a multiplicity of roles, making the social hierarchy difficult to define. Few save the polemic writer Daniel Defoe even attempted to classify the social orders. Based on wealth and consumption, his classification does give some idea as to the composition of the society. He identifies:

1. The great, who live profusely
2. The rich, who live plentifully
3. The middle sort, who live well
4. The working trades, who labour hard, but feel no want
5. The country people, farmers etc. who fare indifferently
6. The poor who fare hard
7. The miserable, that really pinch and suffer want.[9]

Poverty was deeply structured into society, mainly because the subsistence sector of the economy was very small. Almost all social groups, even at the domestic level, were committed to the market in some way.[10] More than half the population were unable to survive on their income, among them common soldiers and seamen, labouring people, outservants, cottagers, paupers and vagrants.[11] These people depended heavily on charity and poor relief to supplement their livelihood.

Throughout the eighteenth century, England was emerging as Europe's most progressive society. Indeed, as Roy Porter succinctly states in his book *English Society in the Eighteenth Century*, of 1982:

> The Georgian century formed a distinctive moment in the making of modern England. It was a society which was capitalist, materialist, market-oriented; worldly, pragmatic, responsive to economic pressures. Yet, its political institutions and its distribution of social power, unlike those of modern times, were unashamedly hierarchical, hereditary, and privileged; economic activity was on a human scale (though often not wearing a human face); change was generally occurring at a pace people could adapt to; custom still enjoyed great authority; and deep-rooted particularism, grounded in community loyalties, shaped what remained a face-to-face society.[12]

Despite their distinctions, England's multitude of communities formed a 'united kingdom'.[13] Apart from being a single national group, subject to one sovereign law, the society shared a common written and spoken language. Communication was possible between all levels of society, creating a public well-informed with regard to political as well as social issues. The common language gave people of all ranks confidence to travel away from their home environments, whether for work or pleasure. Movement within and between rural areas, towns, cities, or even to the colonies, enabled social networks to be extended, cultural horizons broadened and fortunes pursued.

A sense of common identity prevailed among those who wielded economic, social and political power, an 'informal cohesion of the British political elite which was the wonder of Europe'.[14] Linked through the patronage system − a network of beneficial familial, pecuniary or business associations − all agreed upon the 'need to preserve and enhance Britain's position in the world'.[15] However, the efficiency of institutions under state control seemed not to be directed toward this objective.[16] Priority was given to the 'demands of political cohesion at Westminster'[17] rather than to the implementation of reforms to improve the running of government departments − an 'anti-interventionist' philosophy which characterised the government's attitude to social reform in general.[18]

Characteristic of the society as a whole was its 'lack of sharp frontiers between classes' – an open-endedness which permitted both an upward and downward social movement.[19] In this regard, it was less rigid than societies in continental Europe. At the aristocratic end of the scale, no social stigma prevented the landed gentry from engaging in trade or industry. Likewise, no legal impediments prevented an artisan from rising in the social scale, though thresholds were more difficult to cross. Ambition, initiative, determination, and skill were necessary ingredients of success. But special requirements often attached to certain positions and the pervasive bonds of patronage frequently determined whether aspirations were fulfilled.[20]

The careers of Captain James Cook and Governor Arthur Phillip are prime demonstrations of this freedom within the social order. The former was the son of a day labourer, served his apprenticeship under a Whitby coaster-owner and entered the navy as an able seaman.[21] The latter, as a poor boy from inner London, entered Greenwich Hospital School, and later became apprenticed to the master of a Greenland whaler. His demonstrated sea-faring abilities gained him the patronage of Augustus Hervey, a member of a 'noble and influential family, the Earls of Bristol'.[22]

People generally were aware of the fine gradations of the status hierarchy and sought to maximise family and other useful relationships to their own political, social and economic advantage. In the realm of commerce and shipping, one of the greatest assets of any merchant was his connections, especially those with his fellow merchants and master-mariners. Many of the luxury trades established in London in the eighteenth century, such as scientific instrument making, developed within tight networks of family and commercial ties.[23] They demanded skills that needed to be learned, and relied on several other trades for components of the finished product. With commercial sponsorship and patronage, artisans from humble backgrounds, such as navigation instrument makers Jesse Ramsden and John Bird, could become specialists and educators in their field, so achieving higher social status.[24] In theory at least, the gaps between the ranks were bridgeable. There was more room for upward than for downward personal mobility, but the possibilities for movement in either direction helped to mitigate social frictions and to maintain the overall integrity of society.

Foreign visitors to England often deplored the 'fierce' or robust character of English society, its public corruption, ill-manners, insobriety and assertiveness.[25] What impressed them, though, was the nation's fondness for liberty, the independence – sometimes seen as lawlessness – of its individuals and its lack of provincialism.[26] The political and civil liberties which the English regarded as their right gave the society a freedom and openness envied by foreigners subject to more autocratic rule.

The major integrating force of the society was its economy, an interlocking network of markets.[27] Each region of the country specialised in different commodities, rural and urban sectors tending to be complementary. It was a fluctuating economy, affected by seasonal variations but tending to maintain itself in a self-adjusting equilibrium.[28] At the centre of this economic system was London, the hub of domestic market activity and the major commercial link between Britain, the colonies and Europe. London was

> a bottomless pit of consumption...the power-house of politics, law, the Court, fashion, and the arts and sciences...; the forge of luxury industry; the capital of finance...; [and] the greatest port for overseas trade.[29]

By 1780, London was the largest city in Europe, its rapid population growth since 1740 being largely the result of changes in the nature of rural society and the control of epidemic diseases.[30] Young people from the countryside tended to migrate to the city or other centres of industry in search of work, rather than compete for jobs in the new labour-intensive fields of agriculture, and their movement represented a drain on the natural increment in the rural population.[31] Without skills or education, they had difficulty in acquiring remunerative jobs, and many joined the increasing ranks of the 'new poor' – the urban and rural proletariat.

THE NEW WORLD AND BEYOND

England had become involved in the 'commercial revolution' some two centuries earlier, in the wake of the Iberian conquests in the Americas and India in the closing years of the fifteenth century. As European commercial interests switched to the Atlantic and the New World, where rich profits were to be made from American bullion, sugar and slaves, so England sought to expand its trade with Europe, particularly in wool, cloth and wine. Entry into the wider economy of Europe stimulated the development of an English shipbuilding and shipping industry, and better ships and improved methods of navigation gradually enabled English merchants to compete with other European trading nations for trade in the far distant continents of Asia, Africa and America.

Britain's early colonies were established as a direct outcome of private mercantilist enterprise, rather than as a planned government strategy. The potential commercial and political benefits were soon realised, however, and overseas trade and territorial expansion were transformed into national concerns. As an island nation, Britain had a degree of isolation and protection but was vulnerable to naval attack. Maritime exploration and intercontinental communication thus presented a new challenge to age-old conflicts between Britain and other European nations. Improvements in shipping, particularly naval vessels, became essential for the protection of national trade and territory, and for the competition for overseas commerce.

Overseas trade was organised through a number of chartered joint-stock companies, by which means investment capital could be concentrated and financial risk spread between a number of parties. While the government had little interest in establishing direct political control over foreign nations, it might empower the companies to trade with other nations and to settle, conquer, administer and defend their commercial territories.

The continents of Africa and Asia did not readily appeal to Europeans as places to settle, although the luxury goods which these countries supplied found a ready market among wealthier English people. The New World across the Atlantic, with its potentially unlimited resources and proven sea routes, seemed a more attractive place for pioneer settlers. Groups of British and European migrants, for a variety of reasons, established independent communities and private commercial ventures in addition to small trading outposts in North America and the islands of the Caribbean.[32]

The plantation colonies in the West Indies and along the southern seaboard of North America became most highly valued by Britain. African slave labour was used by British estate owners to produce export crops – sugar, cacao,[33] coffee, rice, tobacco and cotton – that

Britain was unable to produce and that were in demand on the European market. Access to these commodities made Britain independent of foreign supplies, and their re-export to Europe boosted Britain's revenue. The traffic in Negroes from Africa was also a highly profitable business.

Merchants employed in the sugar and tobacco trade often carried out convicts to supplement the labour force on the plantations in the Caribbean, Virginia and Maryland. The practice incurred virtually no expense to the government and was beneficial to the merchants and the colonists.[34] The convicts were treated more like 'indentured labour' and once their term of servitude was complete were given a fair opportunity to establish a new life in the colonies, often with considerable success.[35]

The mainland or middle American colonies were primary producers of grains and timber, mainly consumed in the Caribbean and in southern Europe. The New England colonies gave Britain cause for concern: instead of being economically complementary, the New England fisheries and shipbuilding industries, along with rampant smuggling, were directly competitive with British interests.[36] Nevertheless, prior to 1776, American-built ships helped to swell Britain's transatlantic merchant fleets, which numbered thousands by the eighteenth century. Furthermore, New England provided Britain with an additional source of masts and naval supplies for its own shipbuilding industry.

Following the examples of the Portuguese and the Spanish, English trading companies established intermediate bases along the major shipping routes to Africa, Asia and America. Between Europe and India, for example, the British possessed St Helena, and on the Indian continent itself it held Bombay, Madras and Calcutta. In the West Indies, it had Jamaica. Bases were chosen with a view to providing safe anchorages for merchant ships where repairs could be undertaken, food and water supplies replenished, or shelter found from piratical 'commerce-raiders'. However, they did not always fulfil the necessary requirements,[37] so that British ships were frequently forced to rely on the facilities offered by other powers, such as the Dutch at the Cape of Good Hope.

With high profits at stake, rivalries between European trading nations were inevitable. International commerce was seen as a kind of battleground on which nations contended with one another for possession of the precious metals and for profitable employment of their merchants.[38]

Permanent trading settlements and colonies thus became a means of protecting trade monopolies and securing alternative routes of access to sources of commerce, particularly in the Far East. The American colonies had strategic value, as they lay on the western route to China via Cape Horn and the Pacific Ocean.

Although the British government did not directly initiate the early phase of overseas expansion and colonisation, the interlocking interests of various social groups in the seventeenth century gradually transformed a private economic enterprise into a matter of national interest. Local interests were channelled into support for national expansion by parliamentary representatives, who were usually members of the aristocracy with heavy investments in the new commercial ventures. The fusion of various personal and political ambitions, therefore, created a sense of national identity. By the end of the seventeenth century,

> the steady increase in the Commons' interest in a foreign and colonial policy which reflected the country's strategical, economic and religious aims indicated how much expansionism was coming to be regarded as of real national importance.[39]

Each new colony or trading centre became a new economic stimulus for the parent society, providing an outlet for British manufactures and in turn supplying Britain with cash or raw materials for the development and expansion of new trades and industries. Trade in luxury goods was accompanied by a reciprocal flow of ideas. Asian and Oriental craftsmen made wares to European specifications; in turn, English manufacturers learned new production techniques, such as textile dyeing and fine pottery manufacture, enabling them to imitate the imported goods and so create their own markets in these commodities.

Until the innovation of free trade doctrines in the nineteenth century, Britain's commercial policy with regard to its colonies was one of 'Imperial autarky'.[40] Its aim was to ensure that the mother country, with the aid of her satellite colonial economies, could be self-sufficient in war. In a world of competing colonial systems, among which the French seemed especially formidable, sea power was essential for the naval security of England, for maintaining the balance of power in Europe and for protecting overseas interests. To this end, Britain adopted a policy of 'armed diplomacy', a watchful concern for all developments which might have strategic or commercial consequences for the United Kingdom. The government developed administrative and logistical support in the form of a structure of dockyards and provisioning, accounting, recruitment and training facilities for the navy, making it directly responsible to government as an instrument of national policy.

The economic base for sea power, however, did not lie in the colonies themselves. It lay in

> the vitality of national economic life...not with the nation which launches the largest merchant fleet *per se,* but with the state that buttresses the sea-faring prosperity with balanced economic growth.[41]

Monopolies in many of the colonial staples boosted Britain's bullion stocks and affirmed its role as a European middleman, attracting commerce away from France and Holland, its rival imperial powers.

SHIPS AND SHIPPING

The new trade destinations were mostly very distant, and made heavy demands on British shipping. Ships employed in the transatlantic trades usually made one voyage per season, while those trading in the East Indies generally took two to three years to go out to China and back. In contrast, shipping to northern European markets made at least two, if not several, trips per season. The Atlantic trade was not as lucrative as that of the East, dealing primarily with millions of tons of bulky, comparatively cheap colonial staples. It was a great user of shipping capacity, at times utilising more than one-third of the total shipping in foreign trade.[42] Many of the commodities were re-exported in manufactured or raw form to the prize of all markets, Europe. Thus they tied up valuable freight space over extended periods.

Apart from the East Indiamen, many of which were vessels of 1000 or even 1200 tons, the majority of the merchant ships involved in these carrying trades were relatively small. Those used in the West

Indies trade were sometimes as large as 500 tons, but in general ships bound for North America ranged between 150 to 350 tons, the latter being regarded as an 'unusually large ship'.[43] As late as 1788, however, there were only 105 vessels of 500 tons and upwards on the Register of the British Empire, almost all of these being in the East India trade.[44] Large numbers of ships were needed to maintain Britain's overseas and re-export trade; British-owned shipping tonnage rose from 323 000 tons at the beginning of the century to 619 000 tons in 1780 and over one million tons by 1788.[45]

Ships built for one trade often ended up in another, but by and large the first consideration of the designer was the purpose for which he was building. This made for a variety of vessels in use at any one time. The northeast collier barks, paradoxically, had special qualities of strength, stability and handiness which made James Cook choose four – the *Endeavour*, the *Discovery*, the *Resolution* and the *Adventure* for his voyages to the South Seas.

The increased demand for shipping capacity for both domestic and overseas trade stimulated Britain's shipping and shipbuilding industry, especially in postwar periods when losses needed to be replaced. Long-distance voyages to tropical waters subjected vessels to considerable wear and tear, necessitating frequent repairs and overhaul. Innovations in shipbuilding technology, such as the coppering of ships' bottoms as an antifouling device, improved methods of preparing and seasoning timber and the development of air pumps to reduce the dampness in ships' bilges and holds, were all aimed at improving the quality of British ships in the mid to late eighteenth century. New types of cargoes demanded a larger and better class of merchant vessel, and to protect the merchant convoys more effectively the size of naval vessels was steadily increased in keeping with the superior vessels of the French navy.

THE BALTIC TRADE

Britain faced a serious problem: many of the raw materials essential for large shipbuilding and regular ship maintenance had to be imported, if not from the colonies, from the Baltic. The rise of the Baltic trade in the mid-eighteenth century was a consequence of increased shipping requirements created by other expanding trades, particularly transatlantic commerce and the London coal trade.[46]

The Baltic, with its vast timber and marine supplies, was crucial to the political economy of Europe in the age of wooden shipbuilding. It was a source of tar and pitch for caulking, hemp and flax for sails and cordage, copper for sheathing ships' bottoms and high quality Swedish iron for forging anchors. Above all, it was a strategic source of timber for ships' masts and planking.

Much of Britain's steel and bar-iron also came from the Baltic. This was needed by blade-smiths and cutlers for the manufacture of weapons and cutlery, and for the production of other ironware.[47] Iron manufacturing was a significant feature of the eighteenth-century English economy, although exports in 1772 were still insignificant compared with the combined textile exports. Most iron goods – axes, hoes, plough-shares and nails – were sent to American markets, where they were used to extend the colonial frontier. Any disruption in supplies of Baltic iron was likely to spell depression for these industries.[48]

Since the time of the Tudors, attempts had been made to conserve England's timber for shipbuilding, rather than using it as fuel for the smelting of iron and other metals. Mountainous regions of Britain were still thickly forested with firs, and other suitable trees grew on private estates or common land. But the difficulty of transporting timber to markets discouraged cultivators. As England's population increased, there was more profit to be had from agriculture than from woodlands, which tied up money for long periods.[49] Forests were therefore neglected and became almost unproductive of useful timber, especially the 'grown' or 'compass' timbers needed to fabricate hanging and lodging knees and various members of the centreline structure.[50] Small trees felled in the course of land clearance were often suitable for building small ships, but it was the larger vessels which created the major problem, especially the large East Indiamen and the fighting ships of the navy.

The question of timber shortages is generally portrayed as being a naval problem,[51] yet commercial shipping needed timber too. For the merchant marine, there was the added problem that the Admiralty had first call on essential timber supplies. In order to maintain its navy and merchant marine, therefore, Britian had little option but to import timber and marine stores.

Since the Middle Ages, a well-regulated timber trade had

developed in the various Baltic ports, dominated by the Hanseatic League. Hansa merchants exported wool in exchange for deal, used for the construction of London's houses and public buildings.[52] In 1579, the English Eastland Company established trade with the small East Baltic port of Elbing, selling cloth and bringing back cargoes principally of corn. Early in the seventeenth century, some pitch and tar, flax and hemp and a little timber – chiefly masts – was shipped into England from North Russia, Norway and the Baltic. By mid-century the northern European trades had expanded to the point where

> regular demand for Norwegian and Baltic products in England was so great that the Northern trades had come to be leading users of English shipping tonnage . The expansion of the Northern trades never ceased...[53]

Although England had access to colonial mast timber and naval stores (except hemp), colonial trade did not prosper at the expense of the Baltic.[54] Bounties made stores from North America very expensive, but, more importantly, Britain was keen to develop commercial relations with Baltic nations to suppress Dutch trading dominance and expand the market for British manufactures and colonial re-exports.

The Northern trades fell into a number of distinct regions – Norway, Sweden, the East Baltic coasts and the White Sea – each with its own range of commodities. The East Baltic, pioneered by the Eastland Company, was often referred to as the 'East Country'.[55] The southernmost Polish port of Danzig supplied timber, potash and linen goods, Konigsberg and Memel added to these commodities large quantities of flax, and north of Memel the ports served the hemp and flax country. Riga was the principal hemp port, but also provided masts, timber and linen, and the largest flax supplier was Narva. From Riga northwards, the ports were outlets for the products of Russia, even before they came under Russian political control and St Petersburg became a major port. A commercial treaty with Russia in 1734 gave Britain access to Russian iron and enabled England's business with the whole of the East Baltic to expand at 'a pace unmatched, for a time, by that with any other area'.[56]

Until the mid-eighteenth century, regular carriers to the Baltic from England's east coast ports were relatively small, mainly because the total volume of cargoes was not very great and vessels frequently ran the risk of being part-laden. With the rapid acceleration of trade, however, these smaller ships were replaced by a 'motley collection' of larger vessels.[57] Some were especially built to carry timber. In the 1760s, Riga and St Petersburg became

> the resort of many of the largest English ships outside the East India trade – ships of 400–600 tons, which need no longer fear deficiency of cargo.[58]

In 1766, of 100 vessels entering London from northeast Baltic ports, 83 were over 300 tons.[59] London was the centre of the coal and the timber trades, with established facilities for building large vessels.

Dependence on the Baltic trade had certain disadvantages, not the least of which was that it represented a chronic deficit area of trade.[60] The Baltic nations had not reached Britain's level of industrialisation in the eighteenth century and required few manufactures. While they accepted a limited quantity of textiles, Newcastle coal, Cheshire cheese and rock salt, the Baltic nations preferred cash payments, a drain on Britain's bullion resources. Furthermore, the timber trade was controlled by agents of the Baltic suppliers, who were at liberty to divert timber to other buyers, which meant that prices fluctuated according to demand and were often very high.

Supplies from the Baltic were not under British political control, which posed an even greater problem. The Baltic states were liable to be involved in hostile coalitions, in which case The Sound (Öresund) might be effectively closed to commerce. Consequently, once reserve supplies of mast and hull timbers had been used up, 'all British naval strategy might be threatened'.[61] France had allowed its traffic with the Baltic to fall into the hands of the Dutch, who, as 'common carriers', were prepared to transport goods and supplies even for their own adversaries in time of war. If Holland was drawn into any alliance with the Baltic powers, France would thus have unprecedented access to the strategic timber and naval stores.

Britain used its colonies as part of a strategic plan to maintain supplies of essential raw materials and foodstuffs, especially in times of war. But supply was neither assured nor cheap. Even in Canada, access to suitable timber was restricted to that which grew close to the riverways. Although potentially good supplies grew further inland, land haulage was difficult and made felling uneconomical, especially since the timber then had to be freighted across the Atlantic. These factors made Britain ever more reliant on Baltic sources. Reports from agents in the various colonies, and the findings of navigators sent to explore the farther reaches of the world were always considered by government agencies in the light of this unfortunate reliance.

As the American War of Independence proved, even the best of strategic plans could fail: the flow of naval stores from North America very quickly ceased. Britain resumed, in 1778, its habitual maritime interception of neutral Baltic carriers in order to seize enemy stores. The Empress Catherine of Russia provoked a reaction in the form of the Armed Neutrality of 1780, with the aim of protecting neutral shipping rights, and Holland joined the Baltic powers, leaving Britain totally isolated from all its European allies – the 'dominating factor', some believe, for Britain's eventual defeat.[62]

NATIONAL RIVALRY AND OVERSEAS EXPANSION

National rivalries and wars were endemic in eighteenth-century Europe, but were an essential part of the process of expanding overseas trade. Foreign commerce was both lost and created through war. Britain would occupy colonies held by France, Spain or other European powers in order to attack and distract her imperial enemies and to acquire bills of exchange which could be cashed for peace negotiations. In these diplomatic arrangements, British ministers endeavoured, with some degree of skill, to secure colonies which might open up new markets for manufactured goods and retain those which were strategically important.[63] Every war was a check to the development of French commerce. Yet Britain's successes in the War of the Spanish Succession (1701–13) and the Seven Years War (1756–63), would have meant nothing

> but for the peaceful economic and social developments which placed them in a position to take full advantages of those opportunities. Englishmen had learned how to make money breed, and a large part of the accumulated savings of the trading

and business community was invested in foreign trade and the shipping that carried it.[64]

War was a very great drain on resources and finances, but Britain was fortunate in that its early campaigns were fought on the seas or on alien soil, with the aid of foreign and colonial manpower. Apart from shipping losses, therefore, they were not directly destructive of productive strength.[65] Domestic agriculture and industry could continue unhampered, war even acting as a stimulus to certain sectors of the economy, particularly those dealing with government contracts for weapons, ships, uniforms and boots.[66] England was not bankrupted by the wars of the early eighteenth century and endured them more easily than did the other European powers. During the American War of Independence, Britain's economy did not stagnate, but, rather, prospered. New aids to production and distribution enhanced industrial development to the point where a surplus of products such as the world had never seen was accumulating rapidly.[67]

The American war undoubtedly emphasised the strategic problems of fighting overseas campaigns. If inadequate communication systems were one thing, an even greater logistical problem was that 'Every biscuit, man, and bullet required by the British forces in Amercia had to be transported across 3000 miles of ocean'.[68] Furthermore, once the conflict spread to India, the same problem arose there, particularly when the Navy Board was unable to enlist the help of the East India Company to transport troops and supplies.[69] At any one time during the war with North America and the West Indies 322 merchant ships with a combined average tonnage of 96 637 tons were under long-term charter to the Commissioners of the Navy, additional cargo space being rented on a short-term basis.[70]

By securing space on outward-bound merchant ships to the Mediterranean, Canada and the West Indies, the Navy Board could reserve as much transport tonnage as was necessary for the support of the British army in North America. Indeed, short-term charters were often mutually beneficial to the navy and the merchants:

> The use of outward-bound West Indian ships to carry troops to the Caribbean during the American War was truly a marriage of

economic convenience and strategic necessity.[71]

All vessels chartered as transports or victuallers for foreign service were subjected to thorough structural inspection at the Deptford Dockyard on the Thames. Vessels that did not meet the Navy Board's standards were rejected or refitted to comply with particular specifications. Great importance was attached to the height between decks, so that the comfort and health of the troops would not be impaired.

Shipowners were obliged to supply their ships with all the equipment necessary to ensure their seaworthiness, and also had to purchase provisions for the ships' crews and to see that the ships carried the required number of cables and armament. Once a vessel entered naval service, all operational control and risk was surrendered to the Royal Navy, though the master remained responsible for ensuring that the ship was kept fit for service and properly manned.

During the last three years of the American war, the Navy Board found it exceedingly difficult to charter additional ships at reasonable freight rates.[72] It was therefore compelled to invoke its right to refuse to discharge a vessel, and ordered shipowners to repair and refit their ships for further service on their return to Britain.[73]

FOREIGN TRADE AND NEW IDEAS

Britain emerged from the American war having lost its North American colonies but surprisingly little else. It had secured naval control in the West Indies, commercially the most valuable of all the colonies and strategically a base from which to embark on trade to the west coast of America and across the Pacific to China and Southeast Asia. In Indian waters, French assaults had been fended off, and in the Mediterranean Spain had failed to secure its main objective, the return of Gibraltar. Above all, the British Isles and its people, the centre of the Empire's wealth, strength and naval power, were only temporarily affected by the war. Britain emerged as 'a harrassed though not *exhausted* nation'[74] since 'so small a fraction of the country's wealth was collected in taxes'.[75]

By the end of the American war, Britain's wealth had been increased and considerable advances had been made in methods of agriculture, land transportation, iron production, the spinning of cotton and the application of steam power. Britain was poised to take off industrially, but the American economy still depended heavily on British manufactured goods. Following protracted peace negotiations from 1782 to 1784, Britain's flow of finance remained steady and, while there was no postwar boom in exports, there was no depression either.[76] Once peace was established, regular trade with North America and Europe was soon resumed.

While Britain's iron industry, based primarily on the home market, provided the fixed capital for economic growth, other industries, in particular the cotton industry, were heavily dependent on foreign trade.[77] The development of the textile industries had been boosted by capital that flowed on from the sugar trade in the west coast ports, and technological innovations in the latter years of the American war had raised production levels. Profitability, however, was increasingly dependent on the purchasing power of other countries. The circulation of capital now affected trade and industry far more than it ever had and the lack of it brought social and economic hardship to many.

Foreign trade was

> ...the matrix from which sprang modernizing institutions and attitudes...of accumulation, calculation, profit-seeking, investment and maximising...[78]

These attitudes were characteristic of an increasingly commercial and consumerist society and undoubtedly influenced social behaviour and political decision-making in the late eighteenth century. Indeed, the loss of the American colonies led to a considerable revival of thought and attitudes concerning the political and economic value of what was left of the British Empire.

From the mid-eighteenth century, public attention was drawn to the political inequality of society as described by writers such as Rousseau.[79] Concern for human freedom and equal rights gathered force. The adverse aspects of English social life and behaviour were publically condemned by would-be reformers – the question of slavery; living conditions of the labouring poor; the brutality, vindictiveness and uncertainty of the law; and the increasing gap between the rich and the poor.

Many politicians, such as William Pitt the Younger, who was

appointed prime minister in 1783, were well-read in these new philosophies, but the social and political systems were still dominated by an aristocratic elite, closely allied to the wealthy mercantilist class, whose personal commercial interests made them very tolerant of economic enterprises which would boost both profits and national strength. They saw no reason for any change in the hard line they held toward the production of sugar by slave labour, an enterprise on which a massive part of the nation's economy depended.[80] In 1776 and again in 1783, petitions to have the slave trade abolished were rejected immediately by both houses of parliament.[81] Pitt was an open supporter of his old friend and antislavery campaigner William Wilberforce, but he adopted an anti-interventionist stance, preferring to maintain the status quo rather than divide political loyalties. Clearly, the financial benefits to France or the United States of Britain's abolition of the slave trade were sufficient to outweigh the immorality and the dehumanising aspects of this practice.

For the relatively wealthy majority, the pressure for reform was not considered imperative as long as England remained

> a land of economic opportunity, in which the state did not blight enterprise and prosperity…[and]…the long arm of patronage offered loaves and fishes to enough people right down the social scale, and the crumbs of comfort kept others' hopes alive.[82]

Short cyclical periods of intense unemployment exacerbated poverty, but the poorer members of eighteenth-century English society appear to have had an incredible stamina and resistance to social and economic inertia.[83] They worked in whatever capacity they could, when or where jobs were available, relying on cottage crafts and other domestic industries for supplementary income. For those out of work, the family network was the greatest source of moral and economic support.

After the American War of Independence numerous discharged soldiers and seamen swelled the ranks of the unemployed. The navy drew heavily on the merchant marine for additional seamen in times of war, but ordinary sailors and military were generally conscripted vagrants, semi-employed persons or criminals. Some 200 000 men had been taken off the labour market for service during the conflict.[84]

Many young boys had entered the forces before acquiring knowledge of a trade, and consequently re-entered the job market with limited skills. So while there were those who probably had no desire to work, or who preferred to return to their old corrupt ways, there were others who did not have the necessary skills to work, even if they wanted to.

When many of these jobless people were forced to live on poor relief, charity or minimal part-time wages, it comes as no surprise that crime proliferated after the war, especially in the urban areas where the population was concentrated.[85] Violence and crime were common in 1774 when jobs were scarce in the shipping industry, which suggests that crime rates fluctuated throughout the late eighteenth century in response to economic pressures, rather than steadily increasing.[86] Indeed, the supposition that crime increased markedly during this period appears to be unproven.[87]

Certainly, disorder and crime were a feature of early eighteenth-century society and punishment was brutal and severe in the extreme if a conviction was secured:

> Force was used not just criminally, but as a matter of routine to achieve social and political goals, smudging hard-and-fast distinctions between the worlds of criminality and politics.[88]

Crime in the late eighteenth century was still 'a cottage industry, a jumble of individual acts of desperation'.[89] Petty theft, larceny, forgery, poaching, scavenging and other non-organised criminal pursuits were often the last resort for those who could not make ends meet. Conspicuous spending on gin, gambling and luxuries such as tea, sugar or entertainment to distract the buyer from his or her social hardship frequently led to debt and the debtors' prison. A person's standing in the community or the business world was marred by a conviction, and custom made it difficult to re-establish old acquaintances and so acquire one's daily bread.[90] Thus, many people were committed to crime as a permanent way of life.

In the emerging consumerist culture, the social values of personal property, goods and services began to change. People were prepared to condemn any threat to their livelihood or property, whether inherited, achieved, or earned through individual labour or endeavour.

Pitt's prime concern in the aftermath of the war was to reconstruct, peacefully and vigorously, Britain's political economy and to unite and connect a 'shattered empire'.[91] His policy of national revival focussed on the restoration of Britain to its prewar financial position by increasing annual revenue and reducing the national debt,[92] and on establishing new alliances and reforming old friendships with European neighbours, in particular the Dutch and the Prussians, to avoid future diplomatic isolation.[93]

The American war had emphasised that Britain had little hope of conquering French and Spanish overseas possessions unless it was able to distract its rivals from a purely maritime war. A continental diversion that engaged these powers in land warfare was the obvious policy for success. But with a limited number of regular British troops, such a strategy would only be possible with the aid of European allies, supported by British revenue. With the French intent on pursuing a treaty of defensive alliance with the Dutch, which would give France access to Dutch bases in Africa, the Indian Ocean and Southeast Asia, Britain's position in India was under threat.[94]

According to Paul M. Kennedy in his book, *The Rise and Fall of British Naval Mastery*, of 1976, 'There was no wish on Pitt's part for an active foreign policy if that could be avoided'.[95] Nevertheless, Pitt was prepared to support other states to prevent any harmful shift in the continental balance of power and to check attempts to undermine Britain's colonial interests. In the peace negotiations following the American war,

> The British Prime Minister's overriding concern was to retain the nation's commercial and territorial dominance of the Caribbean and India, and, if possible, to strengthen the lines of communication with establishments in these regions, so that they might have the means of recovering their prosperity.[96]

British commerce in India and the East was monopolised by the English East India Company, which by now was also a territorial power in India and carried on an increasingly important trade at Canton, China. In order to strengthen Britain's position in India, the government now sought to change its earlier colonial policy of non-intervention. Many of the East India Company directors were members of parliament, though they did not all share the same political allegiances. Through negotiations between the government and the various company factions, the government of British India was left in the hands of the East India Company, but under Pitt's India Act of 1784, the Crown was given ultimate powers of control over the company's affairs.[97]

The company's commercial interests could thus be safeguarded by British military force, especially against possible territorial expansion by France, who still held trading rights in India. As further insurance against the French in the Indian Ocean, the British cabinet sought to put its diplomatic relations with Holland in the East Indies on a friendly footing.[98] The Cape of Good Hope was the 'key to India', and Britain's access to the lucrative and expanding tea trade with China – especially with the passing of the Commutation Act of 1784, which virtually abolished import duties on tea. Britain's aim was to ensure that Dutch bases at the Cape, Trincomalee (Ceylon), and the Dutch East Indies would fall into British rather than French hands in the event of war.

The Admiralty had always co-operated with private merchants and the East India Company to protect merchant convoys from foreign incursion, particularly in times of war.[99] With Britain's trade routes in the Indian Ocean and the waters of furthest Asia and the Malayan world under threat, and the newly independent United States ready to expand its own maritime trade, Britain needed to consider its future very carefully. If war was inevitable, a secure network of bases with convenient access to ships' masts, timber, naval stores, food, water and other supplies was a high priority.

Britain's economy was already firmly linked to a global network of trade which was highly favourable to expanding export-oriented industries. The pace of industrial development was quickening, and an ever-increasing population needed to be fed. Overseas commerce and national expansion could hardly be neglected.

ANOTHER NEW WORLD?

In 1786, in a rare interlude of peace with France, the British government decided to establish a settlement on the east coast of New Holland. Already proclaimed for the British Crown by James Cook in 1770, this land seemingly offered a favourable climate and natural resources conducive to settlement by Europeans, comparable to the New World colonies. The colonisation of Australia marked the beginning of a new era of national expansion in which the British government rather than private individuals took the initiative. Even so, given Britain's domestic and international situation, and the prevailing cultural attitudes to wealth, prosperity and commerce, such action would probably have attracted little attention had it not been for the fact that the people selected to establish the new colony were Prisoners of His Majesty – the Australian word 'pommy', used to describe an English person, is an acronymic reminder of this fact.

The motives behind the Pitt government's decision to establish a penal colony in New South Wales have been questioned by Australian historians in recent years, if only to remove the 'convict stain' from Australian history and present Australia's past in a more respectable light. Nineteenth-century interpretations, based on Lord Sydney's announcement on 18 August 1786 of the scheme to send convicts to Botany Bay, and its accompanying document, entitled 'Heads of a Plan', presented the view that British politicians merely wanted to use New Holland to alleviate the crowded state of the gaols in the different parts of the kingdom.[100] The official account of the founding of the colony emphasised that Britain's need for a new domicile for convicts was the result of 'the necessary cessation of their removal to America'.[101] The 'convict dumping' theory became a popularly held view of Australian colonisation.

Gradually, however, alternative interpretations began to emerge. In 1952, K. M. Dallas suggested that the additional motive of opening up trade with Asia and the Pacific made more sense, but lack of evidence made many scholars skeptical of this view. Then, in 1966, Geoffrey Blainey proposed, in his book *The Tyranny of Distance*, that Botany Bay had been chosen, not because of its distance from England, but rather as a strategic source of raw materials for the British navy.[102] Lord Sydney's announcement had made reference to the fact that

> ...considerable advantage will arise from the cultivation of the New Zealand hemp or flax-plant in the new intended settlement, the supply of which would be of great consequence to us as a naval power...

> ...furthermore, there was a possibility of procuring from New Zealand any quantity of masts and ship timber for the use of our fleets in India...[103]

Emphasising Britain's dependence on the Baltic for these supplies, Blainey suggested that the choice of Botany Bay 'was too obvious to be spelled out' in politicians' letters.[104] Moreover, he considered flax and timber to be the key to the early settlement of uninhabited Norfolk Island.[105] When Cook discovered Norfolk Island in 1774, during his second voyage around the world in the *Resolution*, he observed that flax plants grew more prolifically here than in New Zealand. Fibres of the New Zealand flax plant (*Phormium tenax*) tested by experts in canvas and cordage manufacture on Cook's return to England, produced impressive results.[106] The island's majestic pines might also provide essential mast timber, the British government hoped.

While Blainey's interpretation provided a plausible explanation as to why Norfolk Island was settled so soon after the First Fleet arrived at Botany Bay, his hypothesis was still founded on very limited documentary evidence and was soon the subject of intellectual criticism.[107] Nevertheless, Blainey's treatment of the subject did much to stimulate a re-assessment of official and unofficial sources and the question gave rise to lively debate in the 1970s.

Some doubt was cast by Geoffrey Bolton in an article in 1978, entitled 'The hollow conqueror: flax and the foundation of Australia', as to whether or not the plan for Botany Bay had been drawn up by Lord Sydney or 'some under-secretary or chief clerk in the Home Office'.[108] It appeared that the plan contained elements of schemes presented to the government two to three years earlier. Historians had to consider these early proposals in greater depth in order to determine whether the British government did indeed have alternative motivations for settling Botany Bay. Initially, attention focussed on schemes presented by James Matra in 1783 and Sir George Young in 1784.[109]

The emphasis given to the benefits for British trade and commerce in Southeast Asian, Eastern and Pacific waters led historians such as H.T. Fry to argue that New South Wales was established to strengthen the security of the East India Company's routes to

Canton.[110] With Britain's annexation of Penang on 11 August 1786, the Bay of Bengal and the Straits of Malacca could be protected, while a settlement at Botany Bay would safeguard the route to Canton via Tasmania that the East India Company had been considering.

Matra's plan suggested that New South Wales would serve as a convenient base for expanded trade with China and islands in the Pacific Ocean. Such trade would stimulate the export of greater quantities of British woollens and manufactured goods to Japan and other eastern countries. It might challenge Dutch commercial monopoly of the Asian archipelago, giving Britain access to the spice trade. If a war with Holland or Spain developed, a base on the east coast of Australia would enable Britain to maintain a check on both these powers. Although Matra does not specifically mention France, that country's ambitions in the East Indies and the Pacific would be of prime interest. So, in the context of Britain's 'swing to the East' to regain its prosperity following the American war, a colony on the eastern seaboard of Australia would have certain economic and political advantages.

Many of these ideas were reflected in the London newspapers of 1786,[111] yet some historians felt that the Pitt government was incapable of making considered long-term decisions. Whether available documents were in themselves a true reflection of political thought and opinion, and the validity of unofficial sources, were also debated questions.[112] A number of scholars began to synthesise earlier arguments in the light of broader searches for documentary evidence.

Among them was Alan Frost, who pursued the question from a thorough investigation of a wide selection of data to arrive at what is currently the leading, though not universally accepted, thesis in the long debate.[113] Frost argues against the 'dumping' theory, believing that such a view assumes that, following the loss of the North American colonies, British administrations of the late eighteenth and nineteenth centuries lost interest in empire. Contrary to the view that the Pitt administration's decision to colonise New South Wales arose from inertia and incapacity, Frost sees it as a positive decision taken in response to the imperatives of Britain's situation in Europe and the East in the mid-1780s.

Not the least of Britain's concerns was the fact that France shared a similar view in terms of foreign policy, that is, that the nation's recovery from the financial stress of the American war largely depended on the maintenance and extension of eastern trade.[114] As peace returned, France was actively moving to strengthen its position in Europe, the Middle East and India. England and France were thus poised for an intense diplomatic struggle.

Frost concludes that the choice of Botany Bay was a well-considered and deliberate decision, one of a series of responses to the French threat. The new base would confirm the nation's claim to New South Wales and increase its capacity to protect its eastern interests. The opportunity Botany Bay afforded of obtaining a more certain source of strategic naval materials for fleets in eastern waters from Norfolk Island, New Zealand or mainland New South Wales was a particular reason why it was chosen in favour of other suggested locations. Britain's main objective was to create a port which, in wartime, would be self-sufficient in food and naval stores, which British shipping could retire to for refreshment and refitting, and from which squadrons might sail to attack French, Dutch and Spanish bases and shipping. It appears, from Frost's work, that questions of naval strategy were the government's prime motivation in establishing a colony at Botany Bay, and settling Norfolk Island: the removal of convicts was only of secondary importance.[115]

THE PREPARATION OF THE FIRST FLEET

A.G.L. Shaw, in his contribution to Crowley's *A New History of Australia*, of 1974, wrote that:

> From the British point of view, the expedition [to Botany Bay] was not a major enterprise, which perhaps explains some of its shortcomings in personnel and equipment.[116]

Certainly, the First Fleet did not leave England amidst crowds of well-wishers, nor did the newspapers of the day give front page coverage to the event. The *Daily Universal Register*, which in 1788 became *The Times*, did not even report its departure from Spithead on 13 May 1787.[117]

A voyage across several thousand miles of ocean to a country still

The convict hulk Incredible: *a cartoonist's impression of convict overcrowding. Illustration by Roland Harvey from Alan Boardman,* Great Events in Australian History, *1985. Reproduced by kind permission of the Five Mile Press.*

relatively unknown could not be undertaken without careful preparation, in which the Admiralty had considerable experience. The transporting of large numbers of troops to America and India during the American War of Independence had alerted the Navy Board to some of the particular problems associated with the use of regular merchantmen as transports, as opposed to the more commodious East Indiamen. There was little difference between the bulk carriage of common soldiers and that of the convicts to be transported to Botany Bay and similar conditions applied with respect to the quality and seaworthiness of the vessels employed for the voyage, their victualling and their manpower.

In addition to the *Sirius* and the *Supply*, the Navy Board chartered six merchantmen to transport the convicts – the *Alexander*, the *Charlotte*, the *Friendship*, the *Lady Penrhyn*, the *Scarborough* and the *Prince of Wales* – and three to carry stores – the *Borrowdale*, the

Fishburn and the *Golden Grove*. All were comparatively new vessels, the oldest built in 1780 and the newest in 1786.[118] Moreover, they had all been constructed in well-reputed shipbuilding centres – Scarborough, Hull, Whitby, Sunderland and the Thames. With tonnages ranging from 272 to 452 tons, the transports and storeships equalled the capacity of some of the larger merchant ships of the eighteenth century, East Indiamen excepted. All were subjected to the navy's rigorous inspection before acceptance, and were fitted out at Deptford under the supervision of Captain George Teer, the Agent for Transports in the Thames, and later Lieutenant John Shortland.[119] It took only ten weeks to get the nine ships ready, and the two naval vessels followed close behind – some reflection of Charles Middleton's efficient naval administration.[120]

Contemporary opinion in general was that the convicts fared rather well. A letter sent to the editor of the *Gentleman's Magazine* from an eye-witness at Shadwell on 4 December 1786 notes,

> ...a strict and marked attention to their well-being, by the respective officers under the Navy Board, both as to ships, provisions, and every necessary that they may stand in need of. To enumerate particulars would be needless; even trifles have been thought of. And when I confess the manner in which they are provided for in their voyage, with the mode which used to be adopted, I hesitate not to assert, that Government have paid a minute attention to them. One instance as a proof: they now have comfortable beds. Formerly, when the convicts were transported by contract to America, there were no beds. Government paid a certain sum, and the contractor took care that no 'luxuries' were allowed.[121]

In the preparation of such a large expedition, some omissions were bound to occur.[122] Some of the clothing for the women convicts was left behind, and the records of the convicts' crimes. The fleet departed without any small arms ammunition on board, despite requests that it be put on board at Portsmouth. On the whole, however, the fleet was well-prepared and government officials had a generally humane attitude toward the 'disagreeable and troublesome business'.[123]

The government's choice of Captain Arthur Phillip to lead the expedition was undoubtedly a humane and enlightened decision. As Alan Frost has admirably shown in his book *Arthur Phillip 1738–1814: His Voyaging*, of 1987, Phillip had broad seafaring experience and personal knowledge of ports and personnel along the route. Moreover,

> ...his humble origins and wide experience of diverse cultures,
> ...had given him something of an egalitarian outlook and a tolerance of people's failings.[124]

Perhaps more important, however, was the fact that he held in contempt those of his countrymen who 'claimed the benefits of English freedom and yet in distant colonies deprived others utterly of their liberty'.[125] In time, Australia came to be viewed as a symbol of the New World – a land of economic opportunity and egalitarian principles – ideals to which Arthur Phillip aspired with regard to the new colony at Botany Bay.[126]

CHAPTER 2

Building and outfitting the *Berwick*

Built for the Baltic trade in 1780 and 1781, the *Berwick* was purchased by the British navy prior to completion and fitted out as an armed storeship. It was a time of stress for the British government, facing defeat against her American offspring, and a great number of British merchant ships were being converted from northern European trading vessels to cross-Atlantic store and troop carriers.

Exploration and settlement on the Atlantic seaboard provided Europe with a frontier of seemingly limitless resources. The Atlantic effectively singled out the British and the French as the principal contenders for these resources. The same applied to the Indian Ocean, while the Pacific, because of its great distance, was not yet an important sphere of trade. Other areas of potential rivalry were the Baltic and the Mediterranean. Baltic ports provided Britain with wheat, iron, copper, tar, pitch, hemp, and masts. More British ships visited the Baltic than visited any other region.

Access to the naval stores of the Baltic was essential for the maritime nations. Thus Europe controlled two oceanic trades, radiating from the Atlantic and the Indian Ocean. Together with these trades was the interchange, by short voyage, of the products of the Baltic and the Mediterranean. The European nations were heavily dependent on their neighbours and the outside world; interrupted communication with sources of supply could spell ruin. Hence the vital importance of sea power.

British ships did not change much during the eighteenth century. Their owners, and hence the shipbuilders, were concerned with the production of efficient vessels to carry the maximum amount of cargo or to provide adequate gun platforms. Safety and weatherliness (the ability to sail close to the wind without drifting to leeward) were required, but proven designs were generally preferred to innovations.[1] There was some increase in the size of vessels and minor changes were brought about in hull shape and rigging. The general introduction, late in the century, of copper sheathing and fastenings, and new applications of iron in the construction and fitting out of

Rotherhithe shipyard, 1793. Painting by Robert Dodd.
PORT OF LONDON AUTHORITY COLLECTION, MUSEUM OF DOCKLANDS

ships, brought great benefits in the early years of the nineteenth century. But most modern maritime historians emphasise a sameness among eighteenth-century vessels. Some even refer to a standard type.

The variation that did exist among merchant ships is most frequently pointed out in relation to the East Indiamen:

> Throughout the [East India] company's life, the ships which took out the bullion and broadcloth and brought back the chintzes and teas were practically indistinguishable from naval vessels. Employed as they were in 'rich trades', carrying cargoes of relatively low bulk and high value without competition, they were not under the same pressure to keep down costs by stowing as much as possible and sailing with the minimum number of hands as, say, the Baltic timber ships and the East Coast colliers, while the constant pressure in Eastern Seas of pirates and enemy privateers or warships required that they be defensible.[2]

There was some degree of specialisation in ships built for the Baltic timber trade, which required unusually large hold capacity. One historian writes:

> Some ships were especially built to carry timber. They had bluff bows, flush decks and ports in the transom and bows for loading. The heavy timber such as oak went in the hold, with the largest pieces of fir on the top of the pile, but timber was also stacked high on deck.[3]

Vessels built for the timber and coal trades were influenced by the roomy, economical Dutch flyboats. The timber trade was the largest of the foreign trades, timber being by far the greatest import by volume, and it often employed ships which were not fit for the carriage of any other goods except coal.

Very few details of the early life of the *Berwick* have been published, and these details have not been questioned by modern historians. The only widely known contemporary account of the vessel's origins come from the journal of Philip Gidley King, Second Lieutenant on HMS *Sirius* during the First Fleet voyage and aide-de-camp to Captain Arthur Phillip. King wrote in his journal soon after the voyage commenced:

> The construction of a Kings Ship not being deemed proper for this Service the *Berwick* Store Ship was pitched on by the Admiralty & her name changed to the *Sirius*, so called from the bright star in ye Southern constellation of the Great Dog. She had been purchased on the Stocks by Government in 1781 & was sent once to America as a Storeship during ye War & once after the peace to ye W^t Indies since which time she had lay'n in ordinary at Deptford, till named for this Service, when she was taken in to dock & as the Yard people said, thoroughly overhauled, however we have frequently had reason to think otherwise, in the course of our Voyage.[4]

King was just as deprecatory of the armed tender *Supply*:

> ... formerly a Navy Transport – her size is much too small for so long a voyage which added to her not being able to carry any quantity of Provisions & her sailing very ill renders her a very improper Vessell for this Service.[5]

Four and a half months out to sea King returned to the subject of the *Sirius'* origins, after a day of rolling seas and the discovery that some of the vessel's top timbers were rotten. In pique, King wrote that the events of the day had

> ... brought the following anecdote respecting the Ship to light. She was built in 178– [King's blank space] in the River & intended for an East country man but in loading she took fire & was burnt to her wales, Government being in want of a burthensome ship to send Stores abroad in, the Navy board purchased the bottom of this Ship, she was taken into dock & ran up with the refuse of the Yard, I have already said she went two voyages as a Store Ship since when she has had no repair as the late Surveyor of the Navy & Builder of ye Yard at Deptford reported her fit for the Voyage to which she is destined, Such is the Ship in which is embarked an Officer, whose reputation as well as that of the Nations, is concerned in the present arduous undertaking...[6]

Modern historians have too readily accepted what King himself described as an anecdote and have also misinterpreted its meaning. Let us deal first with the misinterpretation. M. Barnard Eldershaw's *Phillip of Australia,* written in 1938, seems to be the source of the misinterpretation. It states: 'Originally she [*Sirius*] had been built for the East India Company...'[7] The author took King's 'intended for an East country man' as meaning 'built for the East India Company'. Writers now invariably refer to the *Berwick* as an East Indiaman.

The term 'country trade' was used by British merchants to refer to commerce between ports east of the Mediterranean, and 'country ships' were the vessels, generally built in Indian shipyards, which engaged in that commerce. But the British in the eighteenth century also used similar terms in a more localised sense. The Oxford Dictionary defines 'East-country' as 'an eastern country; in 18th century specifically the region of the Baltic.'[8] In the shipbuilding industry 'East country plank' meant 'Baltic oak or elm'.[9] The British government, in seeking a roomy storeship, would be expected to opt for a vessel built as a Baltic trader rather than for one built as an East Indiaman. The *Berwick* is not listed in Horatio Hardy's *Register Of Ships Employed In The Service Of The East India Company Between*

1760 And 1812.[10] Nor is it to be found among the records in the East India Office in London. The available evidence clearly points to the *Berwick* having been built as a Baltic trader rather than as an East Indiaman.

The second point of interest in King's anecdote is the fire he mentions. There appears to be nothing in the Deptford Royal Dockyard letterbooks to corroborate King's comment. The *Berwick* was carefully surveyed by Deptford officers prior to purchase by the navy, and the comprehensive report has no mention of fire damage. Thus the claim must be regarded as nothing more than a mariner's tale, and in the following discussion we take the view that the vessel was only built once.

Ships took a long time to build in the eighteenth century; figures for eleven ships commenced at Portsmouth Dockyard between 1774 and 1783 show that a minimum of fifteen months was spent on each, and that this could increase to up to fourteen years. It is safe to assume that the *Berwick* was commenced in or before 1780. It was a good time to be building, close to the end of a war in which Britain lost over 3300 merchant ships.

The *Berwick* was built at Rotherhithe, then a shipbuilding village on the Thames adjacent to Deptford. Large ocean-going ships of a high standard were being built there as early as the sixteenth century. The *Mayflower* sailed from Rotherhithe with the first settlers for America in 1620. The earliest mention of the *Berwick* is on 12 November 1781, when officers from the navy's Deptford dockyard reported that they had been on board 'the *Berwick* building in Mr Watson's yard tendered to be purchased' and 'carefully inspected the state and condition of the hull'.[11] The vessel was still on the stocks at that time.

Mr Watson, the *Berwick*'s builder, is probably the same Christopher Watson & Co who built another First Fleet ship, the *Prince of Wales*.[12] Watson launched the *Prince of Wales* on the Thames on 12 August 1786, just in time for it to be added to the expedition as the sixth convict ship. The 333-ton *Prince of Wales* was a square-sterned, three-masted two-decker with a poop deck, quarter galleries and a fiddle head. She measured 103 feet (31.5 metres) long, with a breadth of just over 29 feet (9 metres). The vessel was owned by Cornhill merchant James Mather, and was commanded by John Mason.

BUILDING THE BERWICK

Deptford, established by Henry VIII, was one of six royal dockyards which together formed the largest industrial organisation in England in the eighteenth century. A comparatively small yard by the eighteenth century because of its inaccessibility and the shallowness of the river – a maximum of only 19 feet (5.79 metres) – it was nevertheless very busy in wartime. Hundreds of transports tendered for charter to the government were surveyed, and the greater part of the stores sent out to the foreign yards were handled there.[13] Control of Deptford was in the hands of the Navy Board, among whose responsibilities was the procurement of ships for the Royal Navy. The Navy Board's shipping needs were made known to shipowners and brokers by advertising in the press, by word of mouth, and by posting notices in public places. After a ship had been tendered to the Navy Board it had to be inspected, measured, appraised and fitted out for service. The inspection included drilling holes in timbers and planking or inserting a sharp instrument into parts of the vessel to test the soundness of the hull. The height between decks was measured also; for the comfort of any troops being carried, the Navy Board wanted ships with decks at least 4 feet 10 inches (1.47 metres) apart.[14]

The report on the partly built *Berwick* provides the following information:

Length of hull for tonnage 89'8¾"
Breadth extreme 32'9"
Depth in hold 13'
Burthen in tons 511$^{83/94}$
In hold
    Beams: 5 in number
        - length from 13' to 13'6"
        - sided 11" to 12"
        - do bolts: 9 in number
    Steps for the foremast
        - length 9'
        - sided 1'
        - mainmast length 5'6"
        - sided 1' 8"

Crutches: 2 in number
- length from 10' to 12'
- sided from 11" to 8"

Sleepers 1 each side
- length 12'
- sided 9½"
- bolts: 8 in number

Lower deck framed with carlings and ledges
- length 110' 5"

Beams: 18 in number
- distance from 3'4" to 6'7"
- sided 1'½"
- moulded 1'½"

do kneed at each end with 1 dagger and 1 lodging
- sided 8"
- bolts: 6 in number

Height between the lower and middle decks
- afore 5'9"
- midships 5'9"
- abaft 5'9"

Raft ports: 2 in number
may be made 3' square
- height 1'11½"
- thwartships 2'
- depth 2'

Middle deck framed with carlings and ledges
- length 114'

Beams: 19 in number
- distance 2'10" to 6'11"
- sided 10½"
- moulded 8½"

Kneed at each end with 1 hanging and 1 lodging
- sided 6½"
- bolts: 6 in number

Height
- afore 5'3"
- middle 5'4"
- abaft 6'4"

Ports: 12 in number each side
- height 1'6"
- fore and aft 2'4"
- depth 2'1"
do distance between 6'3"
Upper deck framed with carlings and ledges and flush fore and aft
- length 118'
Beams 29 distances from 1'11" to 6'6"
- sided 9"
- moulded 7"
Knee at each end with 1 hanging and 1 lodging
- sided 7"
- bolts: 7 in number
Timbers to be run up to form the ports 9 each side
- height 2"
- fore and aft 1'9½"
- depth 3'1"
Has a figure head and galleries new.[15]

At the time of the *Berwick*'s completion the tonnage of all new ships of war built for the navy, and of vessels purchased for navy service, was calculated by the following method:

The length to be taken on a straight line along the lower edge of the rabbet of the keel of the ship from a perpendicular or square from the back of the main post at the height of the wing transom to a perpendicular or square at the height of the upper deck and middle deck for 3 decked ships from the fore part of the stem, then from the length between those perpendiculars, subtract ⅗ of the breadth for the rake forward and 2 ½ for every foot the wing transom is high above the lower part of the rabbet of the keel, for the rake abaft, the remainder is the length of the keel for tonnage.

…the main breadth to be taken from the outside of the outside plank in the broadest part of the ship either above or below the wales, deducting from the said thickness of plank all that it exceeds the thickness of the plank of the bottom… so that the moulding breadth or breadth of the frame will then be less than the main breadth so found [by] the thickness of the plank of the

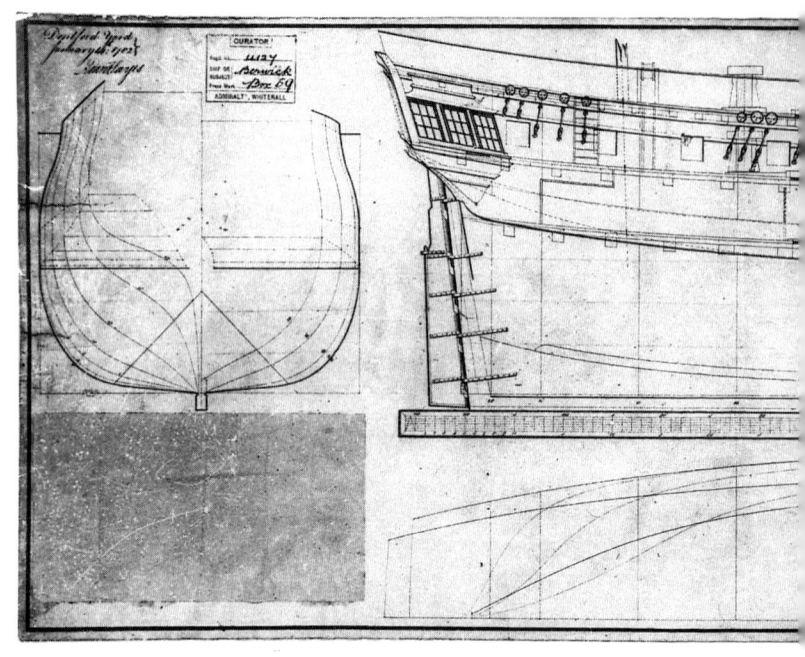

Draught of the incomplete Berwick, *January 1782.*
NATIONAL MARITIME MUSEUM, GREENWICH

bottom. Then multiply the length of the keel for tonnage by the main breadth so taken and the product of the half breadth dividing the whole by 94 the quotient will be the tonnage.[16]

By this method it was possible to calculate the tonnage – a measurement of space within a vessel – before the upper works were completed, applying the formula 'length x breadth x ½ breadth divided by 94' to the figures given in the survey.

At 511 tons the *Berwick* was a large ship for her time. Five out of every six ships owned in Britain at that time were of less than 200 tons.

It is clear from the survey report that the *Berwick* had acquired her most significant structural features before she was purchased by the navy. The upper deck was level fore and aft; East Indiamen also were often built in this way to facilitate the training of troops on the voyage. The extra deck made greater cargo storage possible on a Baltic timber trader, and on an armed storeship it could provide a platform for more guns. The knees in the *Berwick* were, as in other ships of the time, of wood rather than iron.

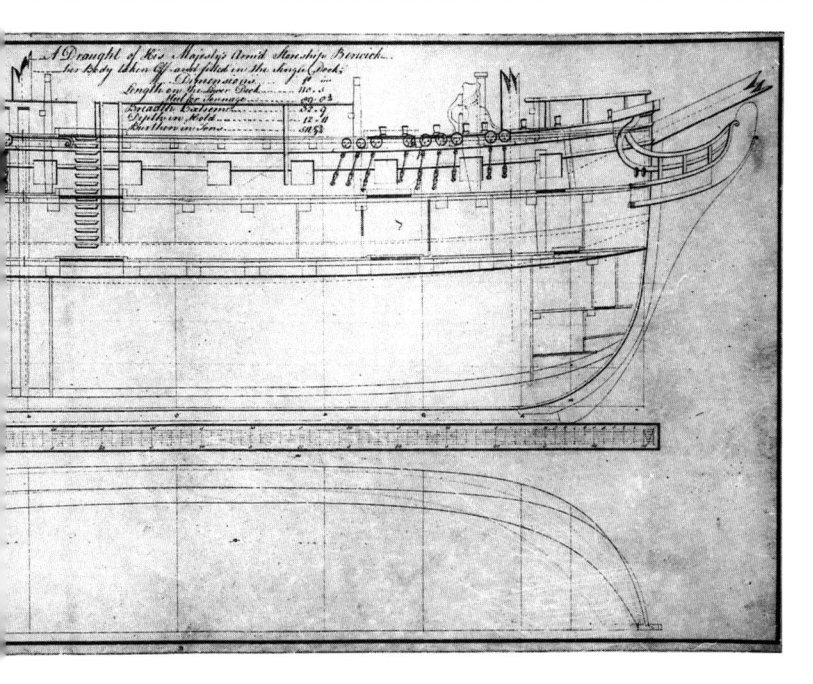

Further information about the *Berwick* can be gleaned from the plans drawn after her purchase by the navy.[17] Plans – draughts – were taken from all purchased vessels and today these are the best source of design information about British merchant vessels of the period. In the 1780s ship types were still classified according to their hulls. The *Berwick* had elements of both frigate and bark hulls. Features conforming with the frigate hull design were the full head, cheeks, rails and figurehead at the bows, and the square tuck, galleries, and wales terminating in the wing transom at the stern. Features more consistent with a bark were her full convex entrance and run.

At the mid section she had flat floors, easy rounded bilges and vertical sides below a sharp tumblehome. One windlass and one capstan are shown on the upper deck, but there are no deckhouses.

The deck beams are shown in the plan drawing, along with the twelve middle deck gunports, but no gunports are yet shown on the incomplete upper deck. Also absent in the draught is the detail of the incomplete upper stern, including the name board, stern windows and associated decoration.

The ratio between the *Berwick*'s keel length and beam, claimed to be a reliable gauge of a ship's sailing qualities in the pre-clipper era, was 3.0:1 – she was a short, beamy, deep vessel with good cargo carrying qualities. In some respects she could be described as a larger version of the collier barks *Endeavour* – with the same keel-length-to-beam ratio – and *Resolution,* vessels earlier chosen by Captain James Cook for his voyages of exploration in the South Seas, or of the armed transport *Bounty* – keel-length-to-beam ratio, 3.0:1 – chosen for the expedition under Captain William Bligh to collect breadfruit plants from Tahiti. The 513-ton, 24-gun HMS *Pandora* sent in pursuit of the *Bounty* – HMS *Sirius* was considered as an alternative pursuit vessel – had a keel-length-to-beam ratio of 3.1:1. The East Indiamen of the time were longer, narrower vessels, built to circumvent tonnage laws which extracted fees from shipowners chiefly on the basis of a ship's beam.[18] Fredrik Chapman's East Indiaman, for example, had a keel-length-to-beam ratio of 3.6: 1.[19]

Before leaving the *Berwick*'s building, reflect upon M. Barnard Eldershaw's claim that the vessel was bought cheaply by the navy and accordingly was of inferior quality. The *Berwick* was purchased for £5856, that is, around £11 10s per ton. This compares with £14 14s per ton for building an East Indiaman of the 800-ton class on the Thames in 1781, considered to be a high price.[20] The *Pandora*, built in 1779 on the Thames by Barnard & Co., cost £10 15s per ton.[21] It is clear, then, that the navy paid a substantial price for the *Berwick* and thus intended that she be a quality vessel.

The bare Baltic trader hull purchased by the British navy in November 1781 required extensive fitting out before she could effectively serve as an armed storeship. The master shipwright at Deptford recommended that the following work be carried out on the hull itself:

> In hold.
>   Abaft port to be cut 2'4" square and well and shot lockers to build.

Lower deck.
> The abaft port to be made large enough to take in a 64- or 74-gun ship masts.

Middle deck.
> And in room of riding bitts to have a windlass and stopper bolts, gratings or hatches to be made and 5 pair of standards against the masts.

Upper deck.
> Flush fore and aft she has no masts, yards or pumps and when fitted as aforementioned, she then will be a proper ship to be purchased for HM Service as an armed storeship...[22]

After her purchase by the navy the *Berwick* was taken into the single dock at Deptford on 1 December 1781 for the work to commence. It is not known what type of timber was used for the completion of the ship, but information is available on timber delivered to the Portsmouth yard in 1781, and it is likely that Deptford would have taken similar timber. At Portsmouth, English oak, elm, and beech were received in the greatest volume, followed by Norwegian fir.[23]

The *Berwick* was coppered early in January 1782. The navy had coppered the frigate *Alarm* as an experiment in 1763, and electrolytic action between the copper sheets and the vessel's iron fastenings had led to its false keel falling off. Despite a lack of understanding of electrolysis, the navy persevered with coppering. In 1780 there was a great drive to copper ships. For the purpose of coppering, the *Berwick* received on board, on 5 January, 12 pieces of elm board, 12 pieces of oak board, and 130 sheathing planks. Then on 11 January she received 19 casks of nails.[24] The materials used in coppering also included the following:

Copper sheets of 32 [ounces], 28, 22
Plates lacquered
Paper cartridge
Composition barrel [Dawson's composition]
Paper thick dipped
Copper nails bright headed
Iron nails for the gripe 20

Iron nails for the gripe 2
Nails for the scuppers 4
Nails for the scuppers 3
Tar
Spunyarn
Oakum white
Battens whole.[25]

The *Berwick*'s hull was painted with Dawson's composition, sheathed with paper and then coppered. The elm board would have been used as sheathing above the level of the coppering. The *Berwick*'s hull, like the hulls of other merchant vessels of her time, had been built with iron bolts as fastenings, and with mixed metal braces and pintles.

Masts and yards for the *Berwick* were made to the following dimensions:

	Masts		Yards	
	Length	Diameter	Length	Diameter
Mainmast	17'7"	23¾"	56'3"	13½"
Topmast	46'6"	14"	42'6"	9¾"
Gallantmast (to the top)	23'3"	7"	29'3"	6"
Foremast	70'7"	22½"	49'6"	12⅝"
Topmast	41'10"	14"	38'2"	9"
Gallantmast (to the top)	20'11"	6¾"	26'3"	5⅝"
Mizen Mast gaff	66'8"	15⅞"	27'4"	7¾"
Topmast	31'2"	8½"	28'	5¾"
Bowsprit	47'10"	22½"	-	-
Cr of Jack Yard	-	-	38'2"	9"
Flying Jib Boom	35'10"	10"	26'3"	5⅞"[26]

The mainmast, foremast and mizzenmast were each made from a single tree, which was the normal practice for vessels of fewer than 64 guns. At that time also the aft sides of the masts of storeships were planked with oak, and the fore sides 'fished' with a long piece of oak, concave on one side, to strengthen masts when it became necessary to carry an extra press of sail, or after damage had been incurred.[27] The sails were ordered to be made on 17 December.

The masts and yards were made by contractors. The shortage of labour and of working capacity in the mast houses of Britain's royal dockyards was acute, so it was common practice to contract for the provision of masts and other materials.

BUILDING THE BERWICK

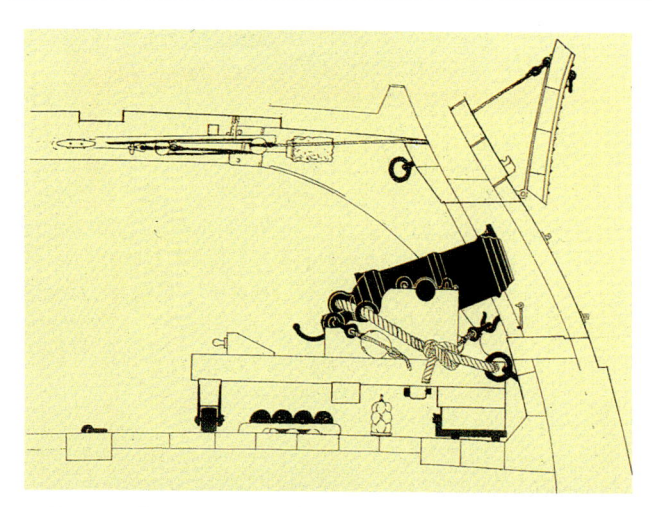

Carronade at gunport, showing grape shot and ball shot. Diagrammatic reconstruction by Jon Carpenter, 1986.
AUSTRALIAN BICENTENNIAL AUTHORITY

The number of guns recommended for the *Berwick* was formidable. On the middle deck she could carry twenty-four 9-pounders, while on the upper deck she could mount six 4-pounders and four 18-pounder carronades.[28]

It seems that fewer guns were taken aboard – other sources indicate respectively sixteen guns and twenty-two guns.[29] It may be that the shipwrights listed the maximum number the vessel could safely carry, and that the number actually carried varied during her time as an armed storeship. Carronades were not counted in rating a ship, except in the case of very small vessels that had carronades on their main decks.

The introduction of carronades in the late 1770s necessitated new systems of mounting. Guns had to be long enough to penetrate the ship's side and allow the muzzle to clear the port lid and any rigging in the way, to minimise the risk of fire. The shorter guns were fitted to the forecastle and quarter deck, where the walls of the ship were thinner. The 18-pounder, one of the original carronades, was a mere 2 feet 4 inches (0.71 metres) long. In September 1781 all ships in the

Royal Navy were ordered to be supplied with gun carriages according to Charles Douglas' invention.[30]

The work of fitting out the *Berwick* progressed rapidly. On 27 December the making of the sea stores was proposed. Then on 14 January the *Berwick* was floated from the dock, to make way for the *Supply*, the vessel that was to become its tender in 1787. The *Berwick* was then ready to receive her 55 men on board. Her draft when ready for sailing was 16 feet (4.9 metres) forward and 17 feet 3 inches (5.3 metres) aft. She carried 80 tons of iron ballast in one-hundredweight pieces, and 40 tons of coals. British warships were classified, according to size and strength, by a rating system. A similar sized 6th rate, the 24-gun *Pandora* of 513 tons, launched in 1779, carried 50 tons of iron ballast and 80 tons of shingle.[31]

It is worth reflecting at this stage upon King's often quoted remark that after purchase by the navy, the burnt out bottom of the *Berwick* 'was taken into dock and ran up with the refuse of the Yard.'[32] We have already observed that the record does not corroborate King's story, written at a time of understandable dissatisfaction about the ship, that the *Berwick* was burnt to her wales. But was the vessel completed using the 'refuse of the Yard', or was this just invention? Relations between yard and naval officers in the late eighteenth century were often strained. One historian has remarked that

> The poor opinion of the dockyards shared by sea officers is not therefore to be wholly trusted. Rather, the circumstances suggest that dockyard officers did well to achieve what they did in spite of numerous problems.[33]

Correspondence during the fitting out of the *Sirius* in 1786 suggests that the *Sirius*' officers had their full share of disagreements with the yard officers at Deptford.

The Deptford Yard management did feel pleased that the work on completing the *Berwick* was done in good time. They wrote on 28 January:

> ... we have employed 2 gangs of shipwright [20 men to a gang] by job [a system of piecework designed for the repair or fitting out of ships] on the *Berwick* Armed Storeship for the sum of £256 and they completed it in 64 single days, by which they gained 2 for 1.[34]

BUILDING THE BERWICK

The job system, designed as an incentive for men to work faster, had effectively halved the time, and cost, that would have been incurred if the men had been working on the 2s1d a day basic wage. This system was frequently used at the time. It was true that the dockyard management in 1781 saw problems about effectively coping with the work given it by the navy. On 27 December they wrote:

> ... the number of labourers No. 335 are too few for carrying on the undermentioned services at this yard... to land and get masts to the pit, launch [ships] for transportation and the contractors, cant [ships] for survey, stow [spars] under the locks... get to hand [materials] for the shipwrights to work on by task... carry and house fishes, cheeks, topmasts yards and tresseltrees, crosstrees, cap etc. To attend the shipwrights on task, unstowing and getting out of berths and carrying to hand for working, moulded timbers, beams, thickstuff... cart rough and sided timber out of piles and get it to pits for conversion, collect from the pits and stow as directed, converted timber, knees, beams, thickstuff, plank, board, caps, crosstrees, drumheads, anchor stocks, chocks, carlings, ledges etc. Land, spread, [and] cart over for survey of, loose plank and deals. Land, attend the survey of and measuring of oak, elm, Wainscott [panelling wood] and Sheaths, board and land on carriages and house the same. Land, attend the surveying and stocking [and] ordering [of] deals. Land and lay for survey spars of all sorts and house the same. Make masts of fir... [stow]... in the ponds. Land and attend the survey of oak and fir rafters. Land, weigh and stack iron ballast and ship do. Land weigh and house ironmongers wares, copper sheet, rolled lead and all species of the lead kind. Load anchors on carts and get them to the smith's shop to be repaired, also get them to the wharf and set up in berths. Get anchors out of berths and... up for stocks. Land, weigh and house cordage, cables, pitch, tar, turpentine, tallow, rosin, varnish, oil etc. Land sails, carry them into the lofts, open and spread them for survey, make them up and stow them in berths. Land, weigh and stack canvas, also lay it on the floor to be measured and mark it up and stow it in berths. Land hammacoes, spread them for survey and stow away do. Land and house slops

and seamen's beds. Land, attend the survey [of] and house engines, blockmakers wares and pump gear. Land stout and stack for survey, also load into carts and to use treenails and wedges. Land, load into carts and pack paving stones. Sweep and clean the yard and ships in dock, and cart away the sullage. Take out of the cellars, break up and melt down and fill with new casks turpentine pitch and tar. Break up and fill into new casks tallow, brimstone and rosin....[35]

Notwithstanding the general shortage of dockyard labour and shipwrights in 1781, there is no evidence to support King's assertion that the *Berwick* was 'ran up with the refuse of the Yard'. Expenditure was as follows:

Hull materials	1553	pounds
workmanship	389	pounds
Masts and yards materials	120	pounds
workmanship	9	pounds
Furniture and stores materials	3707	pounds
workmanship	36	pounds
Total	5817	pounds

This figure compares favourably with £5441 spent on the storeship *Minerva*, £5126 spent on the storeship *Harriet*, and £4061 spent on the storeship *Britannia*, all around the same time.[37] The primary sources then indicate that the *Berwick* was fitted out using materials of the same quality as were used on other vessels at Deptford and other royal dockyards at the time.

Lieutenant Baynton Prideaux went on board the *Berwick* on 21 January 1782 and put the ship in commission. On 25 January he received on board six anchors weighing as follows:

1 x 72 cwt 2 quarters 18 lbs
1 x 69 cwt 3 quarters
1 x 55 cwt 2 quarters
1 x 52 cwt 3 quarters
1 x 33 cwt 3 quarters 14 lbs
1 x 33 cwt 1 quarters 3 lbs.[38]

Of these, only the smallest two would have been suitable for use on board: the rest would have been carried as naval stores. Presumably other smaller anchors were taken on board to work the ship.

A portion of the crew's victuals arrived on 13 February. They included:

> ... 25 bags of bread, 4 casks of beef, 160 tierces [a cask of 190 litre capacity], 2 casks of pork, 160 do. 30 puncheons of beer, 170 litres fresh beef – 2 casks of peas, 15 bushells and 3 gallons – 3 firkins of butter, 178 pounds 2 casks of oatmeal, 15 bushells...[39]

The standard provisions for seamen at that time were slightly more varied: 'Beef, Pork, Beer, Butter, Water, Bread, Cheese, Oatmeal, Peas, Flour, Suet, Raisins, Molasses, Sour Krout, Vinegar, Spirits, Pot Barley, Wine, Candles, Essence of Malt.'[40]

It is clear that the building and outfitting of the *Berwick* were of a high standard when considered in the context of the shipbuilding practices of the eighteenth century. As a Baltic trader her construction was more similar to that of Captain Cook's South Seas exploration ships than to that of the East Indiamen, and this was appropriate for the vessel that was later to be chosen to shepherd the First Fleet to Botany Bay. The *Berwick*'s outfitting, as an armed government storeship and transport, was also consistent with her later role.

Bronze spectacle plate. Photograph by Pat Baker, 1985.
AUSTRALIAN BICENTENNIAL AUTHORITY

CHAPTER 3
Early voyages

The armed storeship *Berwick* sailed on 25 April 1782. Almost immediately her commander, Lieutenant Prideaux, found minor gaps in the work done by Deptford. He wrote to the yard officers:

> ... order some hands down to Longreach, in order to finish several jobs left undone. Also send 14 bolts for muzzle loadings and iron work for fitting 4 rollers, I refer you to the quarter man for the dimensions.[1]

The *Berwick* was initially stationed at the Nore, off Sheerness at the mouth of the Thames. Then she set off across the Atlantic with a convoy, arriving in the still friendly Halifax harbour, Nova Scotia, on 20 August.[2] It was in that autumn that a new British ministry, opposed to the war in America, negotiated a peace. Early in the next year hostilities were suspended by a general armistice, and on 3 September 1783 treaties formally signalled the separation of the independent United States from the British Empire.

The *Berwick* left Halifax on 16 November, again in convoy, and arrived at New York on 7 December. Nothing is known of the *Berwick*'s activities during the following six months. In June 1783 she left New York for Halifax, and she returned to New York a second time before sailing for Britain. She arrived at Spithead in October.

By then she was due for a refit, and she arrived at Deptford for that purpose on 25 October 1783. The coppering of the fleet led to the navy abandoning its previous requirements for annual refits, so more of the maintenance responsibility was passed on to the ships' carpenters.[3] Without regular repair the life of any ship was short. It was claimed in 1812 that 1st rates could run no longer than five or six years without repair and that the average life of the whole navy was no more than eight years. Ships' frames worked and their timbers were liable to be in a constant state of decay from dry rot. Some defects were obvious to the men who sailed the ships, but others were only discovered when the yard officers performed their surveys. Refitting was a complicated procedure in which a ship generally had to be stripped of most of her rigging and all of her guns and stores before being breamed, recoppered and prepared for sea again. These operations were notoriously slow in the royal dockyards, generally taking three or four months.[4] The *Berwick* took over six months.

She was docked on 26 November to have the copper on her bows repaired, a job that only took two days, but

> ... on survey the masts and yards and bowsprit of HM Storeship *Berwick* found the Eaks pieces [wood used to make good a deficiency in length] of the main mast sprung and the mast much worn in the wake of the main yard. I propose to take it out and work a fish on the foreside. The bowsprit is likewise sprung in the bed and as it being of a great length 47' long propose to shorten it at the heel 4' and work a fish at the upper side of it which will be the means of making it serviceable.[5]

While the *Berwick* was being refitted Lieutenant Prideaux wrote an account of how the vessel behaved at sea. This document gives us a rare account of the performance of an eighteenth-century sailing vessel. Today's authors use a variety of criteria for attempting to appraise eighteenth-century ships. MacGregor, in his *Merchant Sailing Ships*, follows Fredrik Chapman's *Architectura Navalis Mercatoria* of 1768 in requiring that a merchant ship ought:

1. to carry a great lading in proportion to its size.
2. to sail well by the wind, in order to beat easily off a coast where it may be embayed, and also to come about well in a hollow sea.
3. to work with a crew small in number in proportion to its cargo.
4. to be able to sail with a small quantity of ballast.[6]

Howard Chapelle, in *The Search for Speed under Sail*, defines a fast vessel as one that in a given state of wind and weather can outsail vessels of the same type, size and rig on at least two of the three basic points of sailing. These points are, with wind dead astern, with the wind abeam, and with the wind ahead.[7] It has been said of an East Indiaman of the 1770s that she

> ... plowed through the water at only 3 or 4 knots in the best of circumstances, half the speed of a contemporary warship... Sailing close to the wind, she made almost as much leeway as headway because the wind pushed her high superstructure sideways like a sail. And worst of all, even in calm waters and with

heavy ballast, an Indiaman was dreadfully cranky, subject to wallowing with an interminable, lurching roll that made all but seasoned mariners seasick.[8]

Judged on the above criteria the *Berwick* comes out well above the average merchant ship of her time. Lieutenant Prideaux gave the following account of her performance:

Query the 1st. How she behaves close hauled and how many knots she runs.
In a top gallant Gale.
- Bears a press of Sail when loaded in General five knots.
- Do when light. Do 6 do.
In a Topsail gale.
- Very easy....
- Moves quick
How she steers, and how she wears and stays.
Under her Reef Topsails - Moves quick in smooth water
Under her Courses - In moving she soon answers her helm and is quick about and makes just little way
And Query, whether she will stay under her courses.
- Doubtful never having occasion to try
2d In each circumstance above mentioned (in sailing with other ships) in what Proportion she forereaches, and in general her Proportion of Lee-way.
- When deep loaded she sails in the General Order of Ships in that Situation. When light in ballast Sails better than Merchant Ships in.general
3d How she proves in Sailing thro' all the Variations of the Wind from its being a Point or two Abaft the Beam, to its veering forward upon the Bow-line in every strength of gale, especially in a stiff Gale and a head sea; and how many Knots she runs in each Circumference, and how she carries her Helm.
- Her best point of sailing is the Wind on the beam in a strong wind...In light winds 6 and 7 knots. She is a favourable ship in a hard sea as she pitches easy.
4th The most knots she runs before the Wind, and how she rolls in the Trough of the Sea.
-She Rolls Deep and knotts as above mentioned.
5th How she behaves in lying Too on a Try under a Mainsail, and

also under a Mizen ballanc'd.
- The Mainsail is her favourite sail as she keeps head way with the helm one horn a Lee and falls off from 2½ to 3 Points.
6th What for a Roader she is, and how she careens.
- She Rides Easy to her Anchors.
7th If upon Trial the best Sailing Draft of Water given as above should not prove to be so, what is the best sailing Draft of Water?
- Afore 14'6", Abaft 15'6".
8th What is her Draft of Water when victualed for six Months, and stored for Foreign Service?
- Afore 16'4", Abaft 17'10".
9th What height is her lowest Gundeck-Port then above the surface of the water.
10th The trim of the ship.
- Eight Inches by the Stern.[9]

The *Berwick* had a speed-length ratio – calculated as a vessel's highest speed divided by the square root of its waterline length – of 0.6, if 7 knots is taken as her maximum speed, but it may be expected that she would have done better than that in heavier winds.[10] How does this performance compare with that of other similar ships of the period? The *Endeavour* was a smaller vessel, but was similar in some respects. Captain Cook noted that 'Her best sailing is with the wind a point or two abaft the beam; she will then run 7 or 8 knots and carry a weather helm.'[11] Her speed-length ratio was thus about 0.8. Cook also observed, 'No sea can best her laying-to under a main sail or mizzen ballanced.'[12] The *Endeavour* made more leeway than most ships, a problem had she been required to sail in convoy.

After her refit was completed the *Berwick* sailed on 7 May 1784. The primary sources give no indication of her whereabouts in the following months. Philip Gidley King states that the vessel went on two voyages as a storeship:

She... was sent once to America as a Storeship during ye War & once after the peace to ye W^r Indies since which time she had lay'n in ordinary at Deptford, till named for this Service...[13]

The *Berwick* may well have travelled to the West Indies in 1784. There was certainly a need for naval stores in the Caribbean at that time. The Treaty of Versailles in 1783 had recognised Britain's loss of power in North American waters and, in a time of ever increasing French naval power, Britain was determined to strengthen her naval security in the Caribbean.

After returning to Deptford on 5 February 1785 the *Berwick* lay in ordinary, effectively out of commission, for much of the next twenty months. Although lying empty and idle, she was not entirely neglected. On 15 April 1785 the Deptford yard was instructed to:

> ... order down 4 water casks to be ready in case of any accidental fire.[14]

In May 1785 the *Berwick* was surveyed afloat and given some repairs, costing £368 for the hull, £337 for the masts and yards, and £2393 for the furniture and stores. The surveyors noted:

> She was built in Mr Watson's yard at Rotherhithe and surveyed 12 November 1781 on the ship the time she was near finished. She has 3 decks and proper raft ports and in our humble opinion she is well built has good room for stowage and is a very proper storeship.[15]

In December 1785 she suffered what was a commonplace in the congested waterway at Deptford:

> .. the *Farmer* West Indiaman, Captain Trew, coming down the river, ran foul of His Majesty's Storeship *Berwick* last Sunday, carried away the Figure of the Head and part of the second upper rail. An estimate to repair the same £5.5.0.[16]

For the time being she was left without a figurehead. Neglected ships were targets for thieves, and in June 1786 three men were apprehended for stealing an awning belonging to the ship.

It is probable that the *Berwick* made another voyage in 1786. On 17 March 1786 the Admiralty passed bills, incurred at or for Madeira – it is not entirely clear that the document refers to the island rather than the wine – for 300 pounds (136 kilograms) of beef and 15 tons of water. It is unlikely that such bills would relate back to her 1784 voyage, or that such a quantity of beef would be required while she lay idle at Deptford.[17] By July 1786 Lieutenant Prideaux had left the ship.

CHAPTER 4
The commissioning of HMS *Sirius*

In July 1786 it must have seemed to the carpenter based on board the *Berwick* that the partly rigged vessel would lie empty at anchor for some time. But events moved quickly. The machinery to implement the British government's decision to found a penal settlement at Botany Bay was put in motion by a letter of 18 August 1786 from the Home Secretary, Lord Sydney, to the Lords Commissioner of the Treasury. The various departmental officials set to work assembling the personnel and vessels for the expedition during the remaining months of the year. Events were put in train at Deptford on 23 August 1786 with orders from the Admiralty to the Navy Board to prepare the *Berwick* to be employed on foreign service.[1]

The Deptford shipwrights responded without delay. On 6 September they proposed:

> ... the following works by job at day 8 [September], 2 tides [a tide was an overtime unit of 1½ hours] this month. *Berwick* Storeship: To complete the fore, main and mizzen masts, and bowsprit, fore and main topmasts and fore and main yards, and all the furniture and spare gear at the prices allowed £88.6.4. To unbolt and take down the head rails, cheeks and timbers, and replace them, trim and fit a new figure or scroll, repair the taffrail, quarter pieces, planipieces [level, or midship pieces], ladders, gratings, and 14 oak shifts [contrivances used for shifting heavy objects about] on the lower deck, 40 deals on the quarterdeck.
>
> 40 men   24 days.   £144[2]

The *Berwick* was docked on the double dock (two docks end to end) on 23 September, to be graved and to have work done on the hull:

> ... By job, in hold, trim and fit a new piece in the raft port, secure the ports of the lower deck, take up and replace 8 shifts of the lower deck and 4 of spirketting, replace the tiller sweep, blocks etc, make new doors, fit the stewards, bread and sail rooms etc and let through scuppers in the openings. Middle deck unbolt and

shift the steps of the bowsprit further aft, shift the coamings and headledges, of standards, nail cants for the officers' berths, fit the spare tiller, hatch bars etc: Upper deck, shift the Planshier, run down new timbers for rough tree nails, trim and fasten blocks and ranges for the rigging, shift the coamings and headledges. With rubboard, take off and replace the fore channel. Backstay stools, lining of anchors, rails, steps, crosstrees, finders, washboards under and fillings between the cheeks. Take off the wood sheathing and damaged copper sheets from the bottom, and drive out some blocks from the hooks.

60 men   24 days   £96[3]

On 4 October the Navy Office was assured that:

> ... the *Berwick*'s fitting is no other than usual, but should anything be directed, you will have timely notice from the Board [of the Admiralty] for so doing.[4]

At this time there had been no specific request for the *Berwick* to be made ready for the First Fleet voyage, but the schedule of maintenance on the vessel indicates that the ship was given a high priority.

The comprehensive refit continued. On 11 October the following work was ordered:

> ... by Task and Job, by day and one tide: In hold take up and fit new limber boards, enlarge the well and shot lockers, fit chocks under the keelson between the floors, drive copper bolts in addition to the iron fastenings, pillar the lower deck beams. Repair and fit a new magazine filling and light rooms, and all the storerooms with bins, shelves, lockers etc. Trim and fasten clamps, get in and knee the orlop, fore and after platforms and lay the same, build a batten bulkhead, and bulkhead in hold and breadroom, make storerooms on the after Platforms, cut out and make 4 hatchways on the lower, middle and upper deck, hatches, ladders etc. Fit the galley, unbolt and replace a pair of riding bitts and crosspieces and standard against them, prepare cants for the officers' berths, cut out air scuttles in them, and wale scuttles down the after platform with ladders etc. Trim and fit a new windlass and capstan, shift the main tier and topsail sheet bolts, crosspieces etc and get out and fit 4 new pumps. Fill the wood

sheathing and cants under the wale, unhang the rudder, make moulds for the braces and pintles, rudder etc and shift several sheets of copper on the bottom, new nail and dress all the copper on the bottom, put up 8 additional deadeyes in the fore and main channels, cut out air scuttles in the officers' cabins, make and hang the lids, all the halfports.

                116 men   10 days   £175

We humbly propose for the quicker dispatch of the [work] shipwrights may be permitted to work 2 tides on the *Berwick* storeship in the room of 1 tide.[5]

Admiral Howe finally wrote to the Navy Board on 12 October:

We... direct you to cause His Majestys Storeship the *Berwick* to be registered on the List of the Royal Navy as a 6th Rate by the name of the *Sirius*, and established with the number of guns and complement of men mentioned...[6]

By this time the *Berwick* had been given a comprehensive overhaul and as a five-year-old armed storeship was in excellent condition. More work, specifically to prepare her for the First Fleet voyage, was ordered on 25 October, four days after her launching from the dock. She was at that time locked alongside the *Carysfort* abreast a hulk:

We humbly propose to perform the following works by job at day and one tide. Storeship *Sirius* Fitting for a Voyage to Botany Bay. To take down the bulkheads on the fore platform, take up the flat of the magazine, get in and knee a beam to lengthen the fore platform, build a bulkhead in the hold, make a head way over the magazine, line and plaster the same, enlarge the storerooms, fit them with bins, shelves, lockers etc, line the breadroom, spiritroom, and fasten the raft port, batten the orlop, build a bulkhead in the afterpart, cut out and make a ladderway to the fore platform and magazine passages, build a sailroom, 2 storerooms on the lower deck, wedge the masts, fit partners round the hand pumps, cut out and make air scuttles through the side on the lower deck, make bins and storerooms, put on locks etc: Middledeck fit new crosspieces to the bitts, fit manger boards and hawsepipes, set up pillars, build bins, lockers etc in the storerooms, partners to the masts, trim and run down timbers, raise the rough tree rails... and works incidental to the rigging and fitting the ship.

100 men   10 days   £125[7]

With the interior work nearing completion the rigging took precedence. First the foremast and bowsprit were rigged, followed by the main and mizzen. Then the fore and aft rigging was set up, and the topmasts rigged. In November the ratlines were attached and the yards and sails set up. The spare sails were brought aboard.

Equipping the *Sirius* for the voyage cost, to 29 December 1786, £2572 for hull, masts and yards, together with £4500 for furniture and stores, a total of £7072. This compares with £3270 spent on the *Supply*, and £730 spent on the transport ships.[8]

An important aspect of the preparation for the voyage was the provision of ballast. Ballasting affects the stability, trim and sailing qualities of a ship. In 1782 the *Berwick* had carried 80 tons of iron ballast and 40 tons of coals, which apparently suited her well. During her preparation for the First Fleet voyage, however, it would appear that Captain Arthur Phillip had more urgent considerations than ballasting the *Sirius*.

The iron ballast or 'Kentledge' of the time consisted of rectangular blocks of several sizes, bearing the king's mark. This form of ballast had the advantages of regular shape and greater weight for volume, a combination which was economical of space and enabled safer, more accurate ballasting of ships. With finger-holes at each end it was also easier for the men to handle.[9]

All ballast was cleared from the *Berwick* during its 1786 refit, and the hold was cleared of dirt. Then 28½ tons of iron ballast was placed back in the hold. To this was added, on 6 November, 70 tons of washed and screened shingle ballast, and 20 chaldrons (some 4½ tons) of coals. The ground tier (lowest level) of provisions barrels was laid in the hold on 10 November, and six days later another 20 tons of shingle ballast was taken aboard. This suggests haphazard loading by Phillip. Commanders of all ships were supposed to follow the ballast plan laid out for their ship, but some ignored this rule. It clearly led to questions from the Navy Board to the Agent for Transports, Captain George Teer, who had to explain on 3 January 1787:

... the proportion of Iron Ballast warranted for the *Sirius* was

80 tons, the quantity supplied her when fitted from hence in 1782, of which they have received but 28½ tons, optional in her Commander, who at the time [it] was taken on board observed if that was not sufficient he would apply for more.[10]

Two days later Teer had more to say on the subject:

... she [Sirius] was governed by no proportion, her supply of all kinds of stores being entirely at the will of Captain Phillip and therefore we did not think it necessary to acquaint you with the ballast he thought proper to take short of what she was before supplied with as a common storeship.[11]

That very day Phillip shifted the spare anchor from the main hatchway and the ground tier of barrels from the main hatchway and around the pumpwell to stow more iron ballast. He took on board an extra 140 pigs (a pig is an oblong mass of metal) of ballast which were placed in the main hatchway, 60 on the starboard side and 80 on the port side.[12] Such an approach to the ballasting of the Sirius did not augur well for her sailing performance on the voyage to Australia. On arrival at Port Jackson, Phillip unstowed the main hold and removed 44 pigs of ballast to the bread room, and 6 to the after hold, to provide a more even distribution of weight.

No ship can survive for long without adequate mooring facilities. Captain Phillip's journal indicates that the Sirius carried four anchors when she embarked on the First Fleet voyage: the best bower, small bower, sheet anchor and spare anchor.[13] The spare anchor was initially stowed in the main hatchway. When the Sirius dragged in heavy weather before departing, Phillip had the two bowers and the spare anchor replaced by three heavier anchors. The anchors were stowed during the voyage.

It is likely that the Sirius carried more than these four anchors. The Supply, for example, was furnished with four 12-hundredweight (610-kilogram) anchors, one 5-hundredweight (254-kilogram) anchor, and one 2½-hundredweight (127-kilogram) anchor.[14] Guns were necessary on the Sirius as a deterrent to the ships of hostile nations and to prisoners contemplating insurrection, and as a means of coping with unforeseen threats upon arrival in New South Wales. The shipwrights had deemed the Berwick capable of carrying twenty-four 9-pounders, six 4-pounders and four 18-pounder carronades in 1781, but it seems unlikely that all of these were carried during her career as an armed storeship, and they would have been entirely removed during the 1786 refit. Her commission stated that the *Sirius* would be armed with four 6-pounder carriage guns, six 18-pounder carronades and eight swivel guns, a very light armament.[15]

On 25 October orders were given to 'fit slides, chocks and iron work for the 18 pounder carronades and plates for 24 swivel guns'.[16] Then on 31 October orders were given to obtain:

> ... 10 more six pounders to be put on board with the iron work necessary for the carriages. Having the iron work the guns can at any time be mounted and may I presume in future be of great use to us on board or on shore, as the service may require.[17]

Orders were given for 200 short land muskets and twelve sergeants' carbines to be supplied to the detachment of marines.

The increase in ordnance requirements was a cause of concern to Agent for Transports Captain Teer. On 4 December he wrote to the Navy Office:

> ... with respect to the guns, camp equipage, tents etc that are ordered from the Tower,... he [Phillip] had not specified and quantity, therefore I cannot judge what room may remain [on the First Fleet ships].[18]

The *Sirius* cast off and made sail downriver for Longreach on 10 December. On the short leg to Longreach a ship drove into the vessel and carried away four of the port side main chain plates.[19] Less than a month later a brig would drive into her and carry away the spritsail yard. The *Sirius* took in her guns and gunners' stores, including powder, on 16 December, and stores for the use of the marines at Botany Bay on 27 January 1787. Two field pieces with ammunition, carriages and firing equipment were received from the transport *Friendship* on 17 March.

HMS *Sirius* was the principal naval consort to the First Fleet, but her role was greater than that. She was required to carry personnel for the penal settlement and her share of provisions and stores for Botany Bay. Deptford was ordered to provide *Sirius* and *Supply* with 'such additional quantities of provisions as they can store'.[20] It was for this additional storage capacity that the navy had selected the armed storeships *Berwick* and *Supply* as naval consorts, rather than purpose-built warships such as the *Pandora*.

A supply of provisions was necessary from the time the first men came on board. There was also food and drink for the voyage and at Botany Bay to be considered. The *Sirius* was to be victualled for twelve months for its complement at whole allowance, with the exception of beer, of which only one month's supply was to be provided because of its limited keeping qualities. Spirits were to be used for the remainder of the period. The full allowance consisted of bread, beer, beef, pork, peas, oatmeal, butter, cheese, vinegar and water.[21]

Provisions for port use came on board on 3 November, and fresh beef was sent on board at intervals. Casks of meat for the ground tier started coming on board on 8 November, and the ground tier had been completed by 10 November as follows: '10 casks beef, 10 casks pork, 17 hogsheads [casks containing 100 to 140 gallons – 455 to 640 litres – of liquids], 8 half hogsheads and 40 barricoes [small barrels of less than 10 gallons – 45 litres]'.[22] By the end of November the water had been completed to 112 tons, and the spirits were on board. Bread and beer came on board on 15 December, and beer supplies were topped up.

In addition to food and drink, a wide variety of stores was required both during and after the voyage. These included wood, candles, lamphorns, tallow, astronomical instruments, spare copper fastening bolts, bosun's and carpenter's general stores, camp forge, copper oven 'fitted with Mr Irving's apparatus for rendering salt water fresh', machines 'for rendering stinking water fresh', and Peruvian bark to be used as a drug for treatment of malaria.[23] Phillip, under pressure to put more men and equipment into the fleet, stowed and restowed items in the *Sirius* :

> 24 December... fixed swinging cranes between decks and removed the carpenters' stores to them.
> 25 December... removed carpenters' stores from forward and stowed them away in the coal hole.
> 28 January... shifted the copper bolts from the carpenters store room to the after hold.[24]

Boats were another source of disagreement between Phillip and the master attendant. A launch and three cutters were among the boats taken on board the *Sirius*. Several of these boats are described in orders:

> ... build one launch 25 feet and one yawl of 27 feet with copper fastenings agreeable to draughts that shall be given, and deliver the same into H M Stores at Deptford in 3 weeks. Deptford Officers to receive the same and appropriate them to the *Berwick* storeship... bill to the contractor at rate of £1.19.0. ...for the launch, including the washboards £1.8.0. ... the yawl, including the bow and quarter boards ... send to Deptford at the first opportunity [for] a cutter of 16 feet.[25]

More boats, disassembled and carried in cases, were intended to be loaded on *Sirius* and *Supply*, but because of the shortage of room were taken on storeships.

The problems of getting all the necessary provisions, stores and equipment into the *Sirius* and the other First Fleet ships continued up to the date of sailing. On 12 May it was observed that:

> ... the provisions and water on board the transports was not completed until yesterday, which prevented our sailing sooner – and now we leave a considerable part of the women's clothing behind us.[26]

The task of recruiting for a ship of war in the years immediately following a substantial period of war was not an easy one. Recruiting for a convict convoy destined for the farthest corner of the globe was an even more daunting task. The ship's muster book gives the details of all the men signed on to the vessel after her commissioning. Captain Phillip started to receive men on 27 October, two days after putting the ship into commission. The ship's complement was originally intended to be as follows:

> 'Captain 3, Lieutenants 3, Master 1, Boatswain 1, Carpenter 1, Gunner 1, Surgeon 1, Master's Mates 3, Midshipmen 9, Surgeon's Mates 2, Captain's Clerk 1, Master at Arms 1, Corporal 1, Armourer 1, do Mates 1, Sailmaker 1, do Mate 1, Purser 1, do Steward 1, Boatswain's Mates 3, Carpenter's do 3, Gunner's do 2, Carpenter's crew 6, Cook 1, do Mate 1, Coxwain 1, Quarter

Masters 6, Quarter Gunners 4, Seamen including servants 79, Marines 22, including Subaltern 1, Sergeant 1, Corporal 1, Drummer 1. Total: 160'.[27]

To this list was added the position of Second Captain, with four servants, to take the command of the ship after arrival at Botany Bay, when Captain Phillip would be required ashore. The servants were to be recruited from seamen already mustered.

Assembling the ship's complement took time. It was necessary to recruit officers from half pay and entice or press able seamen from nearby towns. When the recruiting began the fitting out was still in progress so it was not possible for the men to be accommodated on the *Sirius*. Captain Phillip solved this problem by housing men on the nearby HMS *Flora*, which had recently been paid off but had all the bulkheads, cabins and firehearths still standing. By this means the men were kept out of the way of the artificers working on the *Sirius*, but the officers were close enough to be able to influence the fitting out to their liking. They prepared their victuals on board the *Flora* before their own firehearth was installed on the *Sirius*.

Phillip increased the number of marines to be taken out on the First Fleet, thus incurring the wrath of Captain Teer who wrote to the Navy Board:

> … Captain Phillip has from time to time so increased the orders for stores and implements for Botany Bay, and increased the number of marines from 74 up to 160, I believe I may venture to assure you, they will occupy amongst all the ships, upwards of 300 tons space each day and week, continuing to add more, that I was obliged to put a stop to his wishes still to add…[28]

Having decided how many men were necessary, Phillip next had to acquire them. Progress in 1786 was as follows:[29]

Time when mustered	borne	mustered	chequed	sick
2 Nov	89	86	3	-
9 Nov	101	93	3	5
16 Nov	122	99	3	10
23 Nov	122	107	3	12
30 Nov	139	123	3	13
7 Dec	134	119	6	9

A more detailed account of progress was given on 7 November:

95 mustered
3 widow's men [fictitious men borne in proportion to the ship's company, whose wages were consigned to the officers' widow's pension fund]
4 sick on board
9 officers and servants
89 petty and able
62 short of complement
95 whole number victualled.[30]

Recruiting for a time failed to keep up with the rate of desertion. During the last quarter of 1786 it was recorded that 31 men had 'run' from the *Sirius*. The number of pressed men is not indicated in the muster book, but it seems certain that it was these unfortunates who deserted.

Shortages and difficulties with men were not issues confined to the *Sirius*, but affected the whole fleet. The day before the fleet finally sailed, Phillip remained unsure that the men of some of the vessels were inclined to set sail. He wrote:

> ... the transports having on Friday evening completed their provisions and the wind this morning coming round to the S E, I made the signal to get under weigh, but the seamen on board several of the transports refusing to get their ships under sail, put me under the disagreeable necessity of ordering eight to be taken out of the *Fishburn* and the seamen on board the *Alexander* refusing to proceed to sea, unless they were paid what wages were then due... hope the transports will follow, but they have hitherto behaved very ill... [31]

And so the First Fleet finally set sail. One hundred leagues from the English Channel the *Fishburn* was without five of her crew, who had gone ashore. The *Sirius* was well under her complement of 160, mustering only 136 men at sea in August 1787.

CHAPTER 5

The First Fleet voyage

How the *Sirius* looked during the voyage to Botany Bay is difficult for us to know; most contemporary artists depicted her at a distance or merely as one among a fleet of vessels, and omitted fine detail. Written descriptions of her are limited but it is possible to assemble some details about the vessel's appearance.

After her facelift during the last quarter of 1786 the *Sirius* must have looked smart from keel to truck. Her bottom had been graved, revealing the rich copper colour of her sheathing, old as it was, and damaged copper sheets had been replaced. The wood sheathing higher on her sides had also been replaced. Her dark painted sides bore the popular gold stripe along the main gundeck. The guns themselves were painted black.[1] The Deptford draughts show three side windows on the quarter gallery, and most of the contemporary paintings show her as having five stern windows.[2] Above the stern windows her taffrail exhibited the characteristic gold painted decorative work, and below them a name board would have borne the name *Sirius* in 6 to 8-inch-high lettering.[3]

A new figurehead was mounted on the bows. Several historians have claimed that the figure represented the Duke of Berwick.[4] While this might have been logical for the *Berwick*, it seems odd that the newly commissioned *Sirius* was given a new Duke of Berwick figurehead, although the figurehead did not always have a direct relationship to a vessel's name. Unfortunately the contemporary paintings do not show the figurehead clearly. The figurehead was complemented by white hawse pieces.[5]

On the deck were several roundhouses, low structures not shown in the contemporary illustrations. The launch, nesting its cutter, must also have been housed on the upper deck.

The lower masts were painted, probably with oil, to give them the yellow appearance shown in paintings, while the mastheads and yards were painted black. The broad red-forked commodore's pendant is shown flying from the mainmast in George Raper's illustration of the Fleet at Rio de Janeiro. However, this was not normal:

The Sirius, *drawn by Captain F.J. Bayldon in 1925.*
MITCHELL LIBRARY

despite the size of the expedition, and the presence of a Second Captain on the *Sirius*, the right to fly a broad pennant with the rank of commodore was refused to Captain Phillip in a dispatch from Lord Sydney.[6]

The condition of HMS *Sirius* during the First Fleet voyage belied her appearance, if the journals of some of her officers correctly stated the situation. Three incidents have frequently been cited to support the argument that the *Sirius* was a rotten old tub unsuited to her task. The first was in February 1787, before the *Sirius* had even left Portsmouth. Hunter wrote to Deptford officials that several planks on the gun deck were decayed and required replacing.[7] The second was in August, during the month-long stopover in Rio de Janeiro. On 9 August Phillip wrote of the need for the spar and gun decks to be caulked, commenting that the spar deck had only ever been caulked once, and that both the middle and upper decks leaked badly.[8] These discoveries led Lieutenant William Bradley to write in his journal: 'We have proof already of the great neglect in fitting the ship.'[9]

Caulkers from shore joined men from the *Sirius* and the *Supply* to put this right. The following day Phillip heeled the ship for the carpenter to fix the skirting board that secured the upper edge of the copper sheathing.

The third incident took place in September, during the leg from Rio de Janeiro to Cape Town. Philip Gidley King wrote:

> .... the Ship has labour'd very much which obliged us to house the Guns & lash the ports in fore & aft. A discovery has also been made which tends to prove (if it is necessary) the extreem negligence of the Dock Yard Officers in not giving the *Sirius* the inspection they certainly ought to have done. It being found necessary to rip up the lead which lined one of the Scuttles, the Carpenter in doing it perceived a rotten piece of Wood, which was broke off from one of the Top Timbers, on inspection we found that not only the top Timbers were rotten, but also that many of the futtocks were in the same condition...[10]

These defects should be kept in perspective. Inadequate caulking was a commonplace, and all commanders had to expect routine repairs. Indeed, Navy Board policy was to shift this responsibility from the dockyards to the ships' men:

> When the upper works of ships want caulking do not send artificers from the Yard since it retards the work in the Yard. The crews and carpenters of the ships are to do the work.[11]

The job done under Phillip's supervision at Rio de Janeiro was not carried out properly, and had to be redone several times at Sydney Cove.[12] The leaking upper deck was an irritation to the officers and crew, but it neither endangered the ship nor substantially affected its performance. The hull itself was very watertight. Skirting boards were frequently being lost by all coppered ships; worms ate into the boards because the copper sheathing was not carried high enough beneath them, and they were insufficiently fastened with copper nails.[13] The *Sirius*' carpenter had to redo his own skirting board work in April 1788.

Rotten pieces of wood were the most alarming discovery. The

Sirius was clearly affected by dry rot. Dry rot is influenced by the type and condition of wood used, the environment within the ship – timbers constantly wetted and dried tend to rot faster – and maintenance – air circulation and surface coatings reduce dry rot. Unseasoned timber was frequently used towards the end of the war with America, when ships were urgently required. Ships left unused for a period of time, such as the *Berwick* and other navy storeships, were susceptible to dry rot, and the quality of dockyard inspections in the late eighteenth century was not sufficient to ensure detection of dry rot. Nevertheless, it cannot be claimed that dry rot affected the *Sirius* substantially during the First Fleet voyage. It was a routine maintenance matter on all ships for accessible areas of rot to be attended to by the carpenter.

Captain Phillip did nothing to address the issue of dry rot during his one-month stay at Cape Town, and at Port Jackson his carpenter was employed ashore for months before being allowed to turn his attention to the ship.

M. Barnard Eldershaw described the *Sirius* as 'a bad sailer', and most other historians have agreed that the *Sirius* performed badly during the First Fleet voyage.[14] If speed alone is considered, it could not be argued that the *Sirius* performed particularly well, but she was by no means the slowest in the fleet. Sailing in convoy required only that no ship be much slower than the rest, for a convoy had to stay together for security. The *Supply* was regarded as a faster vessel in light winds and calm seas, but the heavily laden *Sirius* handled the strong winds and heavy seas of the Roaring Forties better than the *Supply* and the rest of the fleet. Contrast her with the *Friendship,* of which diarist Ralph Clark commented 'I never was in a Ship that rold So much as this Ship dose'.[15]

Sailing speed could be gauged over 24 hours by ascertaining latitude and longitude changes with midday sextant fixes and the use of chronometers. The First Fleet travelled at an average of only 3½ knots, but on some days achieved as high as 8½ knots. The 184 days at sea taken to complete the 15 063 miles voyage was nevertheless a very good time for a convoy.

Phillip's decision to split the fleet into two divisions for the final leg of the voyage should not be taken as evidence that *Sirius* was a poor sailer. The important issue in this decision was the difference in speed between the fastest and the slowest transports. The *Charlotte*, the *Lady Penrhyn* and later the *Borrowdale* delayed the fleet. The *Charlotte* had been so slow at the commencement of the voyage that she was towed for several days. On 22 November 1787, before the split of the fleet into two divisions, the strong winds and seas were already showing up the *Supply*'s weakness. Diarist Ralph Clark noted:

> ... the fleet is obliged to Shorten Sail for the *Supply* who is not able to keep up with the fleet as it blows too fresh with a Great Sea running.[16]

King, too, found fault with the *Supply*, commenting that she 'sailed indifferently'. The *Supply* arrived at Botany Bay a mere forty hours before the *Sirius*, and the three transports of the first division gained twenty hours on the *Sirius*.

CHAPTER 6

A voyage around the world from Port Jackson

On the First Fleet's arrival at Port Jackson in January 1788 the establishment of a penal settlement ashore became the first priority of all the officials, and the *Sirius* was neglected in the following seven months. Some very minor maintenance was attended to. On the morning of 10 April the ship was careened for several hours to repair the copper on the bow and to scrub away the accumulated weed 'between wind and water'.[1] For three days in April the carpenter repaired and replaced the skirting board. But at the beginning of May he was directed to the building of huts for women convicts, and he remained on shore for the next six months. A carpenter's assistant and a convict caulker did some caulking of the decks and sides, but without proper supervision they did an unsatisfactory job.

Phillip's first problem was to ensure that the settlement survived. By July nearly 200 men suffering from scurvy had been rendered incapable of doing any work. The recently caulked *Supply* was sent to Lord Howe Island to collect turtle in the hope of checking the scurvy.

In September Phillip made the decision to send the *Sirius* to Cape Town for much-needed supplies. Eight guns, a spare anchor and other items were removed from the ship to lighten its load and provide more space. Thus the ship was left with two or twelve guns, depending on whether the ten extra 6-pounders had been removed with the garrison guns earlier in the year, and three anchors. Hunter set out for Cape Town on 2 October.

Not surprisingly, the *Sirius* performed badly on this arduous 91-day voyage. The vessel had no sooner cleared the harbour than she started to take in water. Hunter had not been instructed by Phillip as to his route to the Cape of Good Hope, and he was attracted to the idea of sailing east, with the wind, around Cape Horn. The alternatives were to sail north around Australia, west towards India and then southwest to the Cape of Good Hope, or to claw back against the wind south of Australia, retracing the First Fleet route across the Indian Ocean. Hunter was interested in the route eastward, and the leak prompted him to choose it in favour of sailing westward. A westward route would have badly weakened men on a salt meat diet, constantly required at the pumps to control a leak. So he set out for Cape Horn, a dangerous passage through ice and storms.

It was necessary to pump the ship every two hours, as it was taking five to six inches of water each hour. After several days the carpenter discovered the leak to be under the fore channel, a little below the surface of the water. The carpenter thought that one of the iron butt bolts had been corroded by the copper sheathing, which had never been taken off since the vessel was first sheathed in 1782. Hunter planned to find and stop the leak as soon as moderate weather allowed him, but the opportunity did not arise until he had arrived at Table Bay, South Africa. Hunter wrote:

> Before we embarked any of the provisions, we heeled the ship, to endeavour to stop the leak, which had kept the pumps so much employed during the voyage, and which I mentioned before, I was in hopes of being able, in fine weather, to get at, and stop at sea; but, after several attempts, we found it impracticable: we were now so fortunate as to get at it; it proceeded from an iron bolt, which had been corroded by the copper, and by the working of the ship had dropped out, and left a hole of more than one inch in diameter. A wooden plug was put in, and covered again with copper. But besides this leak, there were many other smaller holes, which were occasioned by the decay of long spike nails with which the skirting board had been fastened on, and had gone quite through the main plank of the ship's bottom. All were closed, as far as we examined, and the ship for the present made less water, but was not so tight as formerly...[2]

On the voyage to Cape Town, Hunter had seen the result of a problem that had been developing since the *Berwick* was built. It was a problem that all merchant-built ships of the *Berwick*'s period shared. The *Berwick* had been built with iron fastenings and then sheathed with copper. The navy was aware of the inevitable consequences of the resultant electrolytic reaction which corroded the iron fastenings – weakened ships that suddenly developed serious

The Sirius *off Tasman Head, Tasmania, 1788. Wash drawing by George Raper.*
DIXSON GALLERIES, STATE LIBRARY OF NEW SOUTH WALES

leaks in heavy weather – but was not well enough organised or funded to rid its ships of the problem. All ships built for the navy after 1783, and some from before that time – for example HMS *Pandora*, built in 1779 – were copper fastened, and the iron-fastened ships purchased by the navy were sometimes refastened in copper. When the *Supply* was being prepared for the First Fleet voyage, Deptford officials were ordered to

> ... dock and shore the ship, and take out the false keel, drive out the keelson bolts, and all the iron fastenings under the load draught of water and replace them with copper bolts...[3]

Clearly this should also have been done for the *Sirius*. The problem was partially addressed; during the 1786 refit copper bolts were driven in addition to the iron fastenings, so the ship was strongly fastened. Had the First Fleet voyage been undertaken two years earlier this costly procedure would not have been carried out. The partial replacement of iron bolts for the voyage was vital. But the *Sirius* was still subject to sudden leaks when a corroded bolt worked out in heavy weather.

There was concern in the navy in the 1780s about which ships were or were not copper fastened. On 4 September 1786 Edward Hunt, the Surveyor of the Navy, confused by misleading information, wrote to the master shipwright at Deptford asking to be informed as to which, among the vessels described by Deptford as being copper fastened, were actually copper fastened, and which were really iron fastened.[4] On 15 November, in an inquiry regarding bolts used in ships at Deptford it was reported that the *Sirius* was copper and iron fastened, while the *Supply* was copper fastened except for some iron in the deadwood (dry areas in the stern).

Phillip and Hunter were aware of the corrosion problem that might occur on the *Sirius*. A quantity of spare copper bolts was taken on the *Sirius* for the voyage to Botany Bay. Early in that voyage, at Rio de Janeiro, Lieutenant Bradley had experimented with the copper bolts:

> ... while the ship was on the heel to fix the skirting boards, we took the opportunity of driving 2 bolts & 2 spike nails of the white composition [copper alloy] 12 inches below the wale & laid them over with copper, to try if the copper would make any impression on this composition.[5]

All things considered, Phillip had sent Hunter on a dangerous mission, and Hunter, in taking the Cape Horn route, had put the *Sirius'* neglected hull to a severe test. But the test was not yet over. With store rooms completely filled with six months' worth of flour for the whole settlement, twelve months' provisions for the ship's company and various stores for the colony, the *Sirius* left Table Bay for Port Jackson in February 1789.

Towards the end of the voyage, off the east coast of Tasmania, Hunter came close to losing the ship. Having found himself embayed he wrote:

> ... we had every moment reason to fear that the worst might, by the ship striking, launch the whole of us into eternity.[6]

Terrific storms subsequently battered the *Sirius* :

After having weathered Maria's Islands we continued to stand on with a press of sail to the eastward, for I was anxious to gain an offing from the coast, the ship being exceedingly disabled. All the rails of the head, roundhouses, and figure of the head, were washed entirely away; and the rails to which the bumkins were secured were so much weakened as to be required to be frapped down to the knee of the head; the jib-boom, the sprit-sail-yard, and the fore-top-gallant mast were necessarily kept down upon deck to ease the bowsprit, in case any of its securities be in danger from the shattered condition of the cutwater.[7]

The *Sirius* limped into port on 9 May 1789 and the flour was offloaded. In June the vessel was taken across the harbour for repairs to the storm damage and an inspection of the underwater metal fastenings. Provisions and stores were taken ashore, and in August the carpenter and his crew, who again had been attending to the business of the settlement since returning from Cape Town, came back to attend to cutting down timber for the repairs. A survey showed the *Sirius* to be weak in her upper works, a problem to be righted by fixing seven pairs of top riders on each side. Rider timbers were bolted onto ribs to give greater strength. William Falconer observed:

These pieces are rarely used in merchant ships, because they would be extremely inconvenient in the hold, besides occupying too large a space thereof; neither are they always used in vessels of war, at least till after the ship is enfeebled by several cruizes at sea.[8]

The survey also found several decayed bolts under the ship's wales, and the surveyor required an examination of as many of the butt bolts as possible. At the end of October, with all the most urgent work finished, provisions and stores were taken back on board, and in February 1790 the *Sirius* was prepared for sea. By this time she was again in good condition.

CHAPTER 7

Voyage to disaster

By February 1790 the shortage of supplies in the settlement had reached a critical stage. Governor Phillip determined on decisive action. He would send both the *Sirius* and the *Supply* to Norfolk Island with convicts and marines. The *Sirius* would later proceed to China to buy supplies, and Lieutenant-Governor King would make his way to England to put the lamentable state of the colony before the government. The two ships sailed together on 5 March, carrying 116 male and 67 female convicts, 27 children, and two companies of marines – 275 people in all.

The departure of so many is an indication of Phillip's fears. It did not lighten the strain on the commissariat, because these people's rations had to be sent with them to Norfolk Island. But if the time came when there were no rations in the store, those sent to the island would have a better chance of living off the land than those left behind in Sydney.

Norfolk Island, discovered by Captain Cook in 1774, lies in latitude 29.48 degrees south, longitude 167.59 degrees east, about 1500 kilometres from Sydney and 1000 kilometres from Auckland. The island is some eight kilometres long by five kilometres wide. Rising to 300 metres, it is of volcanic origin. Two smaller islands lie on its southern side, Nepean being a low coral-sandstone islet and Phillip a volcanic mass rising to 275 metres. Norfolk Island's coastline consists mainly of high cliffs fringed with pine trees. A kilometre of the south coast is low lying; here is situated Kingston, the second oldest British settlement in the Pacific, founded by Lieutenant Philip Gidley King a few weeks after the establishment of the settlement at Sydney Cove. Governor Phillip praised the settlement in reports, and in 1789 the Secretary of the Home Office stated that 'but for the great expense and labour already incurred at Port Jackson', he might have recommended Norfolk Island as the principal settlement.[1]

After a stormy passage, the *Sirius* made Norfolk Island the morning of 13 March. It was clear that there could be no landing in Sydney Bay, adjacent to the settlement, so Captain Hunter ran round to

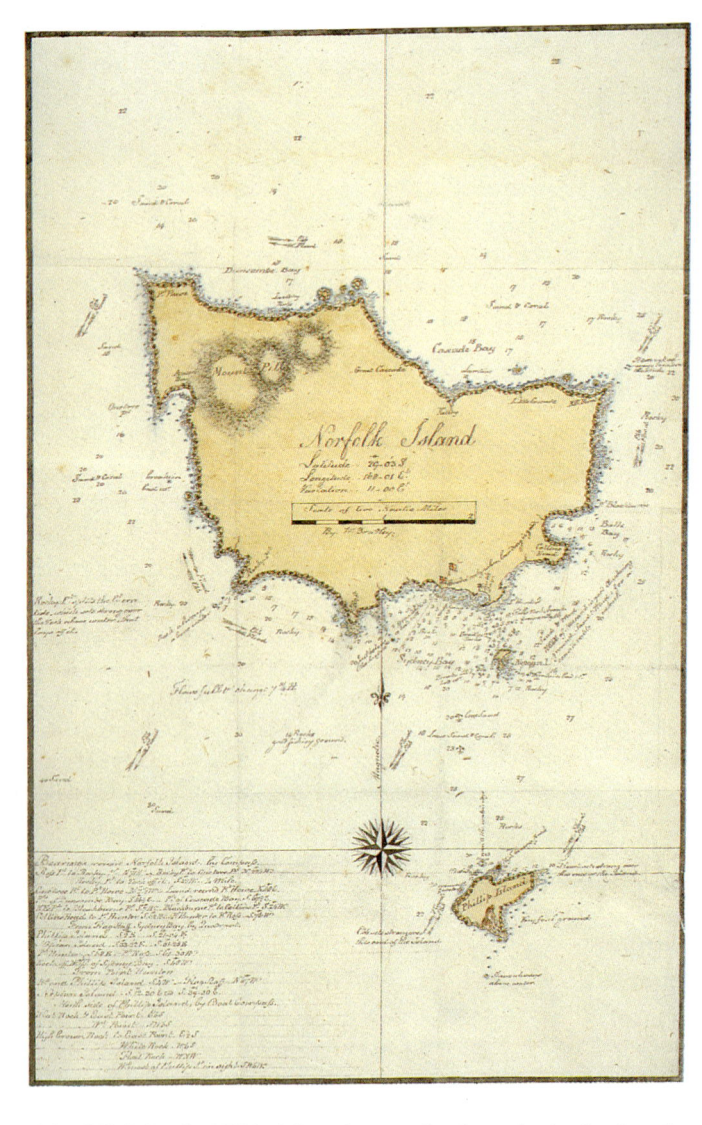

*Norfolk Island, 1790. Map showing lead marks for landing by
William Bradley.*
MITCHELL LIBRARY

Cascade Bay on the northeast side of the island, where he landed all the marines and some of the convicts. The remainder were put ashore on 15 March. With the onset of bad weather the *Sirius* and the *Supply* were then driven out of sight of the island.

On 19 March the gale moderated, and a wind from the southeast brought the *Sirius* close to Phillip Island. Captain Hunter saw the *Supply* lying to the wind in Sydney Bay, and the signal flag on shore which indicated that longboats could land without danger from the surf. Hunter, anxious to avail himself of the very fine landing conditions, stood in for Sydney Bay, came close to the south point of Nepean Island (a kilometre south of the east end of the bay), and soon after 10 a.m. brought the ship's head to the wind, facing out to sea. *Supply* had arrived some time earlier and had already landed all its island provisions.

The *Sirius'* boats had been put down and loaded with provisions when Hunter noticed that his ship was rapidly drifting shoreward. The *Supply* had made sail and Lieutenant Ball called out, waving his hat towards a reef off the west point of Sydney Bay, to warn that the two vessels were drifting perilously close to it. Both vessels set off to windward on a port tack. The *Supply* was ahead, but to leeward of the *Sirius*. At that time, unfortunately, the wind shifted two points (22 degrees 30 minutes) to the south, making it impossible for the ships on their port tack to weather the rocks off Point Ross, the headland projecting from the west end of the bay.

The *Supply* changed to starboard tack and passed just clear under *Sirius'* weather bow. Hunter tried to do likewise, but the *Sirius* failed to tack and fell off the wind, heading again for rocks off Point Ross. Now Hunter's only option was to wear ship – to change to starboard tack by turning the ship's head away from the wind – and endeavour to sail eastward past the landing point and between the east point of Sydney Bay (Point Hunter) and Nepean Island. It was a forlorn hope. The combined forces of the onshore wind and the current made it clear, as they passed the landing, that the vessel would not weather the fringing reef lying some 100 metres off shore. Hunter desperately tried to change tack:

> The helm was again put down, and she had now some additional after sail, which I had no doubt would ensure her coming about.

The Supply *tacks under the* Sirius' *bows off Norfolk Island, 19 March 1790. Painting by William Bradley.*
MITCHELL LIBRARY

She came up almost head to wind, and then hung some time, but by her sails being all aback, had fresh stern way: the anchor was therefore cut away, and all the halyards, sheets and tacks let go, but before the cable could be brought to check her, she struck upon a reef of coral rocks which lies parallel to the shore, and in a few strokes was bilged.[2]

In other words, because the *Sirius* failed to change tack, the wind blew her backwards onto the reef, and she was holed. In one respect Hunter was unlucky: the reef projects seaward in precisely the place where the *Sirius* fell backwards.

The *Sirius* had been put upon the reef not because of any defects in her condition, but as the result of an unexpected shift of the wind, a shoreward current, and, perhaps an overly bold commander. John Bach sums it up well:

The entire episode is a classic text-book example of the gravest of all dangers that confronted the sailing ship; embayment on a lee shore with no sea room to work out. The identical situation had been rapidly developing off the Tasmanian coast when the

The Sirius *trapped on the reef, with supplies drifting ashore, 1790. Painting by George Raper. By courtesy of the British Museum (Natural History), London.*

change of wind, ironically also from the south, had saved the ship. It is unfortunate that such a respected and efficient seaman as Hunter should have twice found himself thus threatened; it is even more distressing for his admirers to find him again involved when he lost the *Venerable* off the English coast. The point, of course, is that the master of a sailing vessel had to get a job done and usually had to strike a compromise between excessive caution and obvious rashness. To put it more bluntly, danger could always be avoided by staying hove-to at sea or by remaining on one's moorings, but in both cases the ship would have been rendered useless for the particular project in hand.[3]

After the *Sirius* struck, the masts were cut away to reduce the stress on the hull, but the heavy surf threw the vessel well in upon the reef. It was clear that the vessel could not be refloated, but Hunter hoped that if the ship were lightened it might be thrown so far over the reef that the people on board could be rescued from the shore. It was then

The rescue operation, 1790. Painting by William Bradley.
MITCHELL LIBRARY

about 11 a.m. All hands were employed in getting provisions out from below, and securing them on the gun deck in case there was an opportunity to float them to shore. As she lay broadside to shore, the *Sirius* made a good breakwater. Two boats were landed with provisions before the increasing surf made further loading impossible. A cable end was floated ashore and secured to a pine tree. A travelling block and hauling lines were then used to pull people, three or four at a time, to the high reef, and from there they crossed to the shore in a small boat. As the evening wore on the tide rose and covered the high reef. The rescue operation was halted for fear that the traveller would foul on the rocks and that people would be drowned. More than half of the ship's company were left on board overnight.

The rising tide did have a positive effect. As the *Sirius* was lifted further inshore the cable attached to the small bower anchor (cut loose before she struck) went taut, and the ship's head was pulled three or four points (33 to 45 degrees) around to face the seas. Now, although she struck violently at high water, at least she lay quiet during low water. The new strengthening riders inserted during the overhaul at Port Jackson helped hold the hull together.

The whole community gathered at the water's edge to witness the disaster. A heartbroken Lieutenant Clark wrote:

> ... the whole of our provisions are in this ship, now a wreck before us, I hope in God we will be able to save some if not all, but why do I flatter myself with such hopes, there is at present no prospect of it, except that of starving, what will become of the people that are on board, for no boat can get alongside for the sea, and here am I who has nothing more than what I stand in and not the smallest hope of my getting anything out of the ship... I am so low that I cannot hold the pencil to write.[4]

The following day the remaining crew got ashore. They reported that the beams of the lower deck had started from the side, and that at high water the sea came to the after hatchway on the lower deck, the bow part of the ship being underwater.

On 22 March the sea moderated and two convicts volunteered to swim to the wreck and liberate the livestock. Most of the animals swam rapidly ashore, including Clark's two sows. Unfortunately the convicts discovered the ship's cellar and were soon gloriously drunk. They set the *Sirius* alight in two places, and before it could be extinguished the fire had burnt through the gun deck.

A state of martial law was declared on the island. The *Supply* sailed on 25 March to deliver the news of the disaster to Port Jackson and seek further supplies. For the next two days the *Sirius*' crew were successful in getting most of the provisions ashore. Every item which came on shore was placed in the care of sentinels until claimed by the owner. Many items were thrown into the water to float ashore, but some of them were lost in the surf.

When the news reached Sydney, Governor Phillip was appalled. He wrote:

> You never saw such dismay as the news of the wreck occasioned among us all; for, to use a sea term, we looked upon her as our sheet anchor [the largest anchor, on which one places reliance when all else has failed].[5]

*The first settlement at Kingston. Watercolour by
Edward Dayes, 1797.*
NATIONAL LIBRARY OF AUSTRALIA

Shortly afterwards Phillip sought permission to leave the colony and return to England.

On Sunday 28 March, a very heavy surf broke the cable to the small bower anchor, and the sea forced the wreck broadside further in upon the reef. Hunter wrote:

> Had she kept in that position she would soon have gone to pieces; but from her being very light forward, the iron ballast having dropped out of her bottom, she was lifted fairly round, and was thrown more than her own length near to the shore, and was, by this change in her position, almost out of the reach of the break of the sea; that is, the surf, which before generally broke upon her, now broke outside, and its force was considerably spent before it washed her; so that when the weather was moderate and the surf low, we got with more ease on board, and could remain there with less danger.[6]

One of the bow ports was enlarged for offloading casks and parcels. For the following two weeks good progress was made in taking goods ashore. The condition of the hull was deteriorating. Many of the knees had broken, and the beams were dislodged from the knees. The orlop deck and the lower deck had given way, and it was dangerous going into the hold. On 10 April a survey was held on provisions saved from the *Sirius*. There were 12 249 kilograms of flour, 5215 kilograms of rice, 47 bushells of caravences (chick-peas), 3798 kilograms of beef, 3631 kilograms of pork and 2513 litres of spirits. Stores included the complete galley, all the spare sails, hawsers, the small bower cable and other unspecified items.[7]

At the end of May the beams and knees were all either broken or loose. At the end of June the vessel was found to be holed the entire length fore and aft on both sides, and the keel had been forced right up into the after hold. The seamen were employed in clearing ground for a garden.

In January 1791 Hunter decided to attempt to salvage the ship's guns. He had previously avoided this task out of concern that the gun deck would collapse upon the orlop and lower decks, preventing access to cables and stores. With the exception of two carronades that had fallen overboard when the masts were cut down, all the guns were hauled ashore with their carriages.

The residents of Norfolk Island were still sorely affected by the *Sirius*' loss in February 1791. Lieutenant-Governor Ross wrote to Governor Phillip:

> With respect to necessaries, not one of them [the detachment under my command] have a shoe to their feet, nor scarce a shirt to their backs; their situation at this juncture is truly deplorable, both men and women having lost almost everything by the wreck of the *Sirius*... The troops are also in great want of cooking utensils; there are but a few small pots among them all, which have been saved from the wreck of the *Sirius*... there is not a pot for every twelve men.[8]

More items were rescued in December 1791. Philip Gidley King listed eighteen copper bolts, six copper sheets, two 7-inch (18-centimetre) cables, 2 hundredweight (90 kilograms) of lead, one fish-tackle fall, 20 pounds (9 kilograms) of chalk, three rudder chains, two top chains, and iron work of various sorts. King proposed sending most of this material to Port Jackson.[9]

The wreck of the *Sirius* finally went to pieces on 1 January 1792, and King reported that everything possible was saved.[10] The hull's ability to withstand the powerful surf for almost two years is an indication that the *Sirius* was a soundly built vessel.

All things considered we must agree with the ship's commander, Captain Hunter, when he observed that the *Sirius* was 'a very capacious and convenient vessel', and 'exceedingly well calculated for such a service [foreign service]'.[11]

Norfolk Island was maintained as a convict settlement for most of the period between 1788 and 1855. In 1852 it became apparent that Pitcairn Island was not suitable for the growing community first established on that island by the *Bounty* mutineers in 1790. Following the withdrawal of the convict settlement from Norfolk Island in 1855, the whole population of Pitcairn, numbering 194, was transferred to Norfolk Island, arriving in 1856. Initially under the control of New South Wales, Norfolk Island became an Australian Commonwealth Territory in 1914, and has since been administered by the Minister for Territories.

CHAPTER 8
The archaeology of the *Sirius*

The last quarter of a century has seen the production of a large number of historical publications about the founding of Australia. Through these works much of the folklore surrounding the convict era has given way to a more rational understanding of the nation's early years. As the previous chapters have shown, the synthesis of various forms of documentary sources continually provides new evidence with which to contest existing interpretations of past events and present new alternatives.

While historians burrow through old manuscripts from the depths of library vaults or other repositories, archaeologists search elsewhere for their data. They collect a different kind of information about the past: tangible, physical evidence of human activity. Whether the material remains exist on land or under water makes little difference to the overall goal of archaeology, which is to increase existing knowledge of past social, cultural, economic and technological phenomena. The fundamental differences between land and maritime archaeology lie in the techniques used for locating sites and recovering data.

Any archaeological investigation involves three principal components: theory, method and analysis. Theory relates to the particular research problem and the rationale, purpose and point of view adopted in order to arrive at a solution; method is the strategy the researcher uses to collect information; analysis involves the preparation and presentation of data, statistical procedures and other techniques which enable inferences to be made with certain degrees of probability.

Archaeology frequently provides information that has not been recorded in written documents, being overlooked by the recorder, or deemed inconsequential. Used in conjunction with historical sources, therefore, archaeological information may confirm, expand upon, or contest the documentary evidence. Thus, archaeological investigation is both a means of testing the validity of facts derived from historical documents and of generating new hypotheses. On the other hand, written sources help to give archaeologists a better idea of the historical background of the material they are dealing with and of the 'organisation' to which it formerly belonged. History and archaeology can be integrated in research into the past, leading to a more holistic explanation and understanding of historical events. This inquiry into HMS *Sirius* is able to draw on both documentary and archaeological sources of information.

Maritime archaeology – the archaeology of ships and seafarers – was established in Australia in 1963, as the result of the discovery of the wrecks of two seventeenth-century Dutch trading ships off the Western Australian coast. Both ships carried large quantities of silver coin, were historically significant and had obvious archaeological potential. To protect the sites from a looter who was destructively using explosives to retrieve bullion and other artefacts, the Western Australian government took legislative action in 1964 to protect all ships wrecked before the year 1900.

The Western Australian Museum, given the responsibility for managing the sites, put into effect an extensive field survey programme and carried out excavations on the sites under greatest threat: the wrecks of the Dutch trading ships *Batavia* (1629), *Vergulde Draeck* (1656), *Zuytdorp* (1712), and *Zeewijk* (1727). The remains of the raised wooden hull of the *Batavia* have provided new information about seventeenth-century merchant ship design and construction, and the collections from these sites have given archaeologists fresh insights into aspects of seventeenth and eighteenth-century trade, navigation and warfare. A number of wrecks from Australia's colonial period were also under threat from souvenir hunters and several of these – the British cargo ship *Eglinton* (1852), the ex-slave ship *James Matthews* (1841), the American China trader *Rapid* (1811), and the British whaler *Lively* (around 1810) – were excavated.

The Commonwealth Government passed its Historic Shipwrecks Act in 1976, and this encouraged other states to develop maritime archaeology programmes. As in Western Australia, field survey has been a predominant aspect of the work done in South Australia, Victoria, Queensland and Tasmania. The three eighteenth-century sites off the east coast of Australia – the rum trader *Sydney Cove* (1797) off Tasmania, the British warship *Pandora* (1791) off

Reconstruction of the hull timbers of the Batavia. *Photograph by Pat Baker.*
WESTERN AUSTRALIAN MARITIME MUSEUM

A diver takes readings of the corrosion activity of objects on the seabed. Photograph by Pat Baker.
AUSTRALIAN BICENTENNIAL AUTHORITY

Queensland, and the *Sirius* off Norfolk Island – have attracted considerable attention from maritime archaeologists.

In the early years of Australian maritime archaeology, preservation of historic shipwrecks, for public education and exhibition purposes as well as for research, was the predominant concern. Questions were formulated – when did the wreck occur? what was the nature of the ship and cargo? who were its crew and passengers? – but the emphasis was upon careful, systematic excavation, aimed at collecting as much information as possible, rather than a single-minded pursuit of the answers to these specific questions. Now that reference collections have been established, however, researchers are able to adopt more explicit problem-oriented approaches to archaeology. Some researchers have realised that total excavation of sites, which demands considerable support facilities, is not the only way to achieve meaningful results. Survey and limited excavation can often provide the answers sought, while a programme of cultural resource management can protect archaeological sites for future archaeologists to pose more enlightened questions.

Maritime archaeologists use shipwrecks to study ships and seafaring. The archaeologist observes the static array of anchors, cannon, pottery sherds, ballast stones and other objects, lying in concentrated or widely dispersed areas on the seabed. From this apparent chaos – the archaeological context – the archaeologist endeavours to create some sense of order in the hope of understanding the highly organised and dynamic assemblage of artefacts that once formed a functioning ship – the systemic context.

How does all this relate to the *Sirius*? The known information about the ship, the sequence of events related to its wrecking, and the early salvage operations have already been outlined. What should be considered now are the physical variables which may have had a direct or indirect effect on the amount, integrity, spatial distribution and state of preservation of artefact material remaining on the seabed.

In a recent study on Quaternary coastlines and submerged prehistoric sites, oceanographers P. Masters and N. Flemming saw the following factors as favouring the preservation of cultural material:

1. A sheltered low energy environment, protected from waves and currents, e.g., within an estuary or sheltered bay, in the lee of islands or headlands, within a karstic [limestone] cave, or at the head of a submarine canyon.

2. Environments which, although exposed to high energy (waves or currents) are protected by adequate sediment cover, (e.g. equilibrium beaches, marshes, wind blown sand).

3. A sequence of events which first buries the site in sediment, and then exhumes it gradually, e.g., covering by terrestrial sediment, followed by submergence, followed by slight wave or current action.[1]

The chemists at the Western Australian Maritime Museum's Department of Materials Conservation look at these environmental parameters from a different perspective.[2] They see the site temperature as of major importance, largely determining the rate of deterioration of both metallic and non-metallic objects. Associated with the temperature is the level of dissolved oxygen on the site, that is, whether the site is fully aerated, partly aerated, or anaerobic. Levels of oxygen determine the corrosion mechanisms and modes of decay. The level of pollution from, for example, sulphides, is related to these factors. Salinity – dissolved chloride from the water being of major importance – affects glass and ceramics as well as metals. The pH level (acidity) of the water affects microenvironments under concretions. Marine organisms form protective concretions around objects belonging to the wreck. The distribution of artefacts influences the effect of their electric fields, iron for example giving cathodic protection to silver, copper and brass.

Another study by maritime archaeologist Keith Muckelroy examined the following environmental attributes with a view to measuring their correlation with the quality of archaeological remains:

A. Exposure to varying physical forces.
   1. Maximum offshore fetch [the length of open water across which the wind is blowing] within 30 degrees of the perpendicular to the coast.
   2. Sea horizon from the site; i.e. sector within which there is more than 10 kilometres of open water.
B. Exposure to specific physical forces.
   3. Percentage of hours during which there are winds of Force 7 or more from directions within the sea horizon.
   4. Maximum speed of tidal streams across site.
C. Water depth.
   5. Minimum depth of site.
   6. Maximum depth of site.
   7. Depth of principal deposit on site.
D. Seabed topography.
   8. Average slope of the seabed over the whole site.
   9. Underwater topography: the proportion of the site over which the seabed consists of geologically recent sedimentary deposits.
   10. Nature of the coarsest material within these deposits.
   11. Nature of the finest material within them.[3]

The study found seabed topography to be the most significant determinant of wreck site condition, followed by exposure to varying physical forces. Correlating these determinants with site condition, Muckelroy graded twenty wreck sites into five classes.

The *Sirius* fits into Muckelroy's Class 5, the worst site category, for which he predicts no structural remains, no organic remains, and only a few scattered objects.[4] The seabed beneath the principal deposit of the *Sirius* consists of a flat calcareous rock platform. Isolated fissures contain boulders. In all but the deepest of these fissures the sea has scoured out any loose sand. Some small pockets of coarse sand have found their way into crevices between the more tightly packed boulders. The seabed topography between the principal deposit and the shore consists of a fringing reef that dries at low tide, and a lagoon. Inside the lagoon flat calcarenite and coral gardens at the western end give way to a sandy bottom, overlying coralline debris, towards the eastern end. It was already clear to Lieutenant-Governor King in March 1790 that the sand was highly mobile. He wrote:

> It is somewhat remarkable that the beach in Sydney Bay has at times five feet of sand on the stones, and at other times it is all cleared away.[5]

In certain storm conditions some of this sand is carried out to sea over the *Sirius* site and back again.

The open sea horizon from the *Sirius* wreck is between 60 degrees and 120 degrees, depending on whether the scattered reefs to the southeast and southwest are taken into account. These small pinnacles do little to reduce the sea movement into the bay. The frequency of storms from the south, combined with the long fetch (to Antarctica and beyond) produces very large swells in Sydney Bay. The shallowness of the water (1.5 to 6 metres), and the substantial seabed slope of the stranding site and principal deposit (8 degrees) results in much of the wave force striking that area. The high energy environment did not augur well for the potential of the *Sirius* site.

Material has been reclaimed from the *Sirius* site at irregular intervals since 1792. The general location of the wreck was never forgotten, as it was shown on charts of Sydney Bay. Throughout the nineteenth century one of the anchors remained visible on the wreck site at low tide, and it was of great interest to visitors to Norfolk Island. In 1905, New South Wales politician Sir Francis Suttor, wanting to make his mark in Australian history, decided that the exposed anchor should be brought to Sydney and placed by Arthur Phillip's statue in the Botanic Gardens.[6] Suttor wrote to the Norfolk Island Administrator, Captain Drake RN, asking if it would be possible to recover the anchor. Captain Drake initially replied that the sea conditions presented too many difficulties, but in June 1905 he announced that the anchor had been blasted free of the seabed and towed alongside the pier ready for shipment to Sydney. Drake had played upon the financial obligations of the island's Methodist Church to the church in Sydney. He offered the church a £20 reward if it could accomplish the raising of the anchor. The story was later told:

> The Administrator provided the explosives and eight men went out at low tide and tried to blast away the rock. These men were Cornish Quintal (captain), Tilly Adams (diver), Marsh Adams, Fysh Adams, Eustace Christian, Johnny Jackson, Dan Buffett and Nicolas Quintal. They reported that they were unable to raise the anchor that day. That night a prayer meeting was held and the anchor was landed on the pier by 10 o'clock next morning. The £20 reward was paid.[7]

The anchor arrived at Sydney on the Burns Philp steamer *Induna*. When Sir Francis saw the 4.6-metre, rusting mass of iron he changed his mind about its exhibition potential, and proposed consulting with the Royal Australian Historical Society about an alternative place for it. It now lies in Macquarie Place. Both flukes and the original ring are missing, detached presumably when the anchor was blasted free of the reef.

Several Norfolk Island residents and Australian Broadcasting Commission cameramen revived interest in the *Sirius* site in 1965. Diving just seaward of the surf zone they saw copper fastening bolts, rudder and sternpost fittings, copper sheathing tacks, lead shot and four anchors. The seawardmost anchor, a 4.62-metre piece, was freed by local divers Ian Kenny, Peter Ely and others and raised by the Wellington-registered SS *Holmburn* in February 1973. The *Holmburn* came so close to the reef that she touched bottom, and, although she was not damaged, her master was reputedly dismissed on return to New Zealand. The anchor was sent to the Western

The Sirius' anchor being lowered into a lighter in 1973. Photograph by Ian Kenny.

Australian Museum for treatment and then returned to Norfolk Island.

Numerous smaller items were raised by resident and visiting divers during the late 1960s and early 1970s. Some of these items are described later in this book. Individual divers are not known to have raised artefacts from the site in more recent years.

Material has also been added to the *Sirius* site since the vessel was

Tom van Leeuwen chipping concretions from the Sirius' *anchor ring. Photograph by Pat Baker, 1985.*
AUSTRALIAN BICENTENNIAL AUTHORITY.

wrecked. Documentary sources indicate that a number of ships were injured or wrecked in Norfolk Island's waters, and some of these might now feasibly be confused with wreckage from the *Sirius*.

The first known accident to a substantial vessel in Sydney Bay occurred on 5 March 1789. Lieutenant-Governor King wrote that the surf was too high for boats to land. The brig *Supply*, anchored in the bay, parted her anchor cable in the heavy weather and her crew were unable to recover the anchor.[8] Its locality today is not known. Oral tradition has it that some years ago a ship named the *Stella Maris* took at least a dozen anchors from the bay to Noumea. Anchors recovered from the seabed are a popular garden decoration on Norfolk Island, and a badly corroded old plan anchor of the type lost by the *Supply* was noticed in a hotel garden by members of the 1983 *Sirius* Project expedition.

Shipping casualties were numerous at Norfolk Island in the nineteenth century, but the vessels involved were generally small, and surviving details of the incidents are generally sketchy. In July 1835 the two-masted schooner *Friendship*, of 89 tons, was wrecked on the reef near the landing place at Kingston. The vessel carried government stores from Sydney, and had been moored on a buoy laid down by the government, but the mooring chain broke during a gale. While one report states that the vessel went to pieces when she struck the reef, another claims that she was washed over the rocks into the 'boat harbour', and that hopes were retained that she might be repaired. *Sirius* Project members did see a length of chain running shoreward towards the Kingston pier, but no other material could be linked with the *Friendship*. The only other early nineteenth-century wreck was the *Fairlie*, reportedly wrecked somewhere on Norfolk Island in February 1840.

Later nineteenth-century wrecks include the 40-ton cutter *Bittern*, which in 1868, while waiting to load cattle for New Caledonia, snapped her anchor at the crown, went into the breakers, and was soon battered to pieces.[9] Two substantial wrecks occurred in May 1873, one on each side of the island. The schooner or brigantine *Diout*, carrying cattle from New Caledonia, parted her chain cable, drifted onto the rocks at Cascades and was totally wrecked. The 217-ton Melbourne-registered whaling barque *Mary Hamilton*, calling at Norfolk Island for wood and water, struck a rock near Nepean Island and was holed. Jacob Christian and other islanders manned the pumps, discharged the barrels of sperm oil into another whaler and helped the crew to run the vessel ashore near the Kingston pier, where, two days later, heavy surf split her in two.[10] The remains, consisting of iron deck supports, copper fastenings and clay bricks, are located 150 metres west of the Kingston pier, and were surveyed by *Sirius* Project expedition members. In June 1893 the 68-ton schooner *Mary Ogilvie* drifted on to the rocks while leaving Emily Bay and soon broke up.[11]

A number of wrecks and strandings are recorded during the twentieth century. These include the 78-ton ketch *Warrigal*, last seen off Phillip Island in April 1918, the Sydney yacht *Iris*, as the result of a wind change when lying close inshore at Kingston, the yacht *Ho Ho* which stranded, the 255-ton, three-masted auxiliary schooner *Renaki*, which was thrown up on the reef on the east side of Kingston pier in 1943, the LFB *Norfolk*, burnt in 1947 at

*Second settlement buildings and the pier, Kingston, 1983.
Photograph by Pat Baker.*
AUSTRALIAN BICENTENNIAL AUTHORITY

Headstone, the LFB *Blue Fin*, wrecked in 1946 at Cascades, the yacht *Rangi*, lost in 1950, and the fishing boat *Matai*, lost in 1967.

Most of the above wrecks are too small, or occurred too late or in the wrong area to have in any way 'contaminated' the *Sirius* wreck. However, one clearly identifiable *Sirius* item was found among the *Mary Hamilton* wreckage, and such items as copper fastening bolts are common to both sites. Iron mast-hoops from the *Renaki* lie almost directly inshore from the *Sirius* site, but these pieces are clearly not from the *Sirius*.

Institutional interest in the *Sirius* site began in 1982, when Jennifer Amess from the commonwealth department responsible for the administration of the Historic Shipwrecks Act – then the Department of Home Affairs and Environment, now the Department of Arts, Sport, Environment, Tourism and Territories – proposed a bicentennial *Sirius* Project as a part of which 'the remains of the ship would be raised as a reminder to all Australians of the country's European origins.'[12]

The bower anchor is transported to deeper water. Photograph by Pat Baker, 1985.
AUSTRALIAN BICENTENNIAL AUTHORITY

The Australian Bicentennial Authority provided funds and announced in 1983 that it was planning a survey to determine what remained of the wreck, and that 'if the ship's remains merit salvage, a full scale operation could be mounted and artefacts restored for exhibition'.[13] This marked the beginning of the *Sirius* Project. The Department of Home Affairs, which initially ran the project, asked the Western Australian Museum to loan personnel to examine the seabed where the *Sirius* was wrecked and to interview residents, and then to report on the condition of anything that remained. Graeme Henderson and Pat Baker from the museum joined Jennifer Amess of the department on a visit to Norfolk Island for a week in December 1983, during which time sea conditions allowed for brief examination of one of the underwater sites on three occasions. Guided by Norfolk Islanders Ian Kenny and Peter Ely, Henderson and Baker snorkelled twice and used aqualungs once.

On the basis of this exploratory fieldwork and such assessment of the historical literature as could be carried out in Western Australia, Henderson, the leader of the project team, produced for the funding and administering departments a report containing tentative identifications of known shipwreck sites at Norfolk Island, and a preliminary register of previously recovered *Sirius* material. The report also contained statements on the cultural significance and conservation policy for the *Sirius* remains and plans for future work.[14]

Australia ICOMOS (the International Council on Monuments and Sites) adopted the Burra Charter in 1980 and this document is now generally referred to by archaeologists with regard to conservation matters. In the terms of the charter, cultural significance means aesthetic, historic, scientific or social value for past, present or future generations. The *Sirius* site is and has been a focus of national sentiment, and thus has social value. It also has great historic value because of the central role played by the *Sirius* during the First Fleet voyage and the establishment of the first settlement at Sydney Cove. The remains of the first Government House at Sydney, built in 1788 and the first major permanent structure erected in Australia, have been described as the most exciting archaeological find of European civilisation in this country.[15] The remains of the *Sirius* must be accorded a similarly high degree of significance in accordance with the ship's role in bringing Europeans to Australian shores.

The scientific or research value of the site did not initially appear to Henderson to be high: little material was exposed, and the flat calcarenite seabed seemed to offer very limited potential for buried remains. The site had potential for a testing of the Muckelroy model of the relationship between environment and site condition. It also offered the opportunity to explore site formation processes generally. The wreck and the salvage operations were momentous events on Norfolk Island, and Henderson thought that assessment of the location of the wreck, and of material remains, would add to the understanding of these events. He considered a number of other broader historical questions. How did the *Sirius* compare, in construction, fitting out, arming, provisioning and manning, with other vessels sent out to the Pacific by Britain and France in the late eighteenth century? Were vessels such as the *Endeavour*, the *Resolution*, the *Bounty*, the *Sirius*, the *Pandora*, and the French *Boussole* and *Astrolabe* essentially different from one another, or did they have many common characteristics? And what was the *Sirius*' condition – was she a suitable choice for the voyage to Botany Bay? The expected dearth of material, however, prevented the project team from persevering at that time with these broader questions at the wreck site.

In planning for the future of the *Sirius* site the project team considered a range of matters. The Department of Arts, Heritage and Environment, and the Australian Bicentennial Authority were concerned to ensure the site's security, given its cultural significance. Some exposed material on the *Sirius* wreck site was being damaged by the environment, and other exposed material was very vulnerable to damage. And the Norfolk Island government, which already had access to the Norfolk Island Historical Society's collection of *Sirius* material, had for some time planned to reopen a museum at Kingston dealing with the history of the area, including the first settlement phase.

The *Sirius* Project adopted the following strategy:

1. Recommend to the Department of Arts, Heritage and Environment that the site be declared under the Historic Shipwrecks Act, 1976. This would mean that material could not legally be removed from the site without a permit from that department.
2. Plan for the removal of exposed material thought to be at risk. Such material would then be treated by conservators and made available both for study and for exhibit in the planned museum on Norfolk Island. The register of material raised from the site prior to the bicentennial *Sirius* Project was to be further developed.
3. Advise the Norfolk Island government on the longer term conservation and housing of the collection.
4. Increase immediately, by public lectures and workshops, the level of awareness within the Norfolk Island community of the cultural significance of the site.
5. Increase public awareness over the long term, through publications and communication with the printed, voice and visual media.
6. Complete the site survey to develop a data base and look at site formation processes. Crucial to the understanding of these processes on the *Sirius* site was the location of the principal deposit.

White water over the wreck site. Photograph by Pat Baker, 1987.
AUSTRALIAN BICENTENNIAL AUTHORITY.

In 1985 the ABA arranged for Henderson to take a twelve-person expedition to Norfolk Island to survey the known concentrations of wreckage from the *Sirius* over three weeks, and search for the principal deposit – the place where the wreck finally went to pieces in January 1792. Jennifer Amess joined the project as representative of the Department of Arts, Heritage and Environment. The Western Australian Museum loaned to the project Henderson, Baker (in charge of photography), Myra Stanbury (in charge of registration) and Dr Ian MacLeod (in charge of conservation). Maritime archaeologists Paul Clark and Mark Staniforth were loaned by their institutions, the Tasmanian National Parks and Wildlife Service and the Victoria Archaeological Survey. Dr David Millar (medical officer), Terry Arnott (in charge of equipment), Lieutenant Tom van Leeuwen (his assistant), Paul Brown (divemaster), and Karen Atkinson (diver) were honorary members of the expedition. The services of expedition members were given freely.

Expedition divers, assisted by volunteers on Norfolk Island, surveyed the known underwater remains using trilateration, a simple

THE SIRIUS

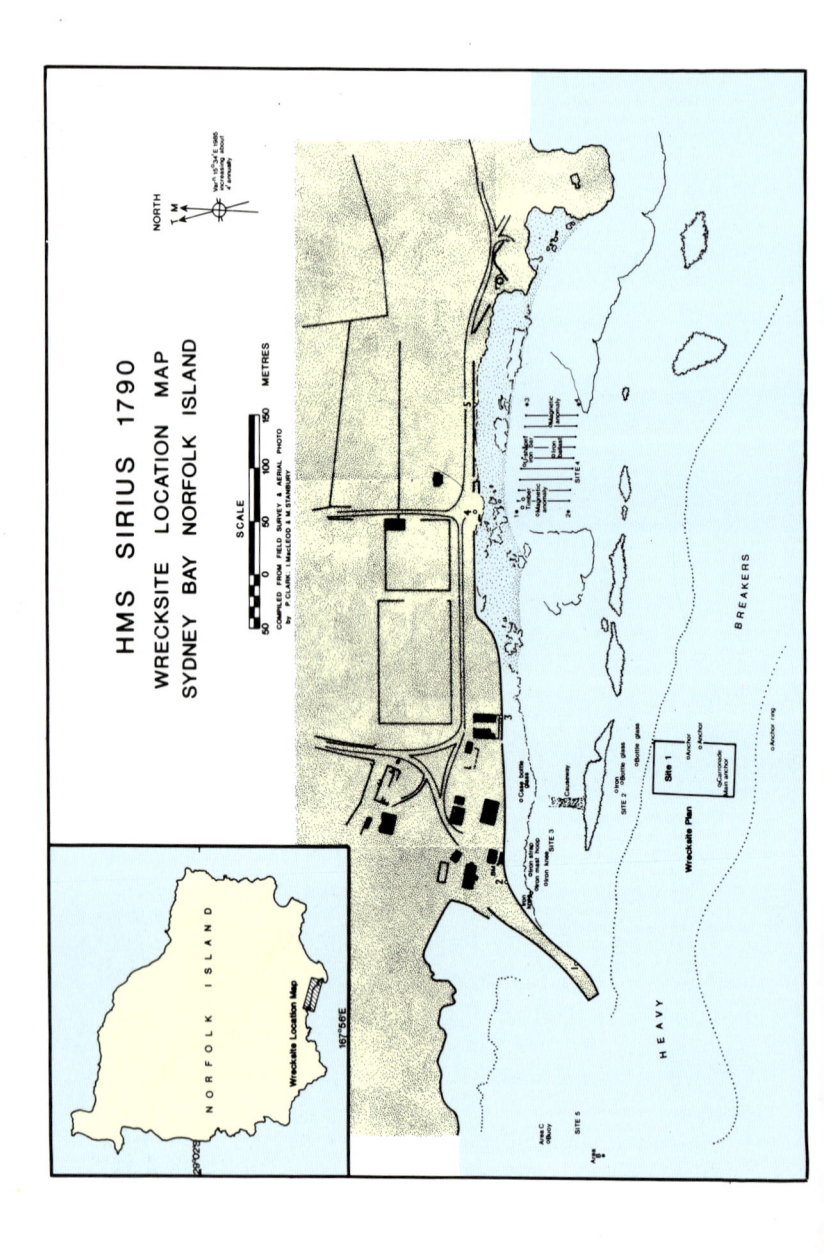

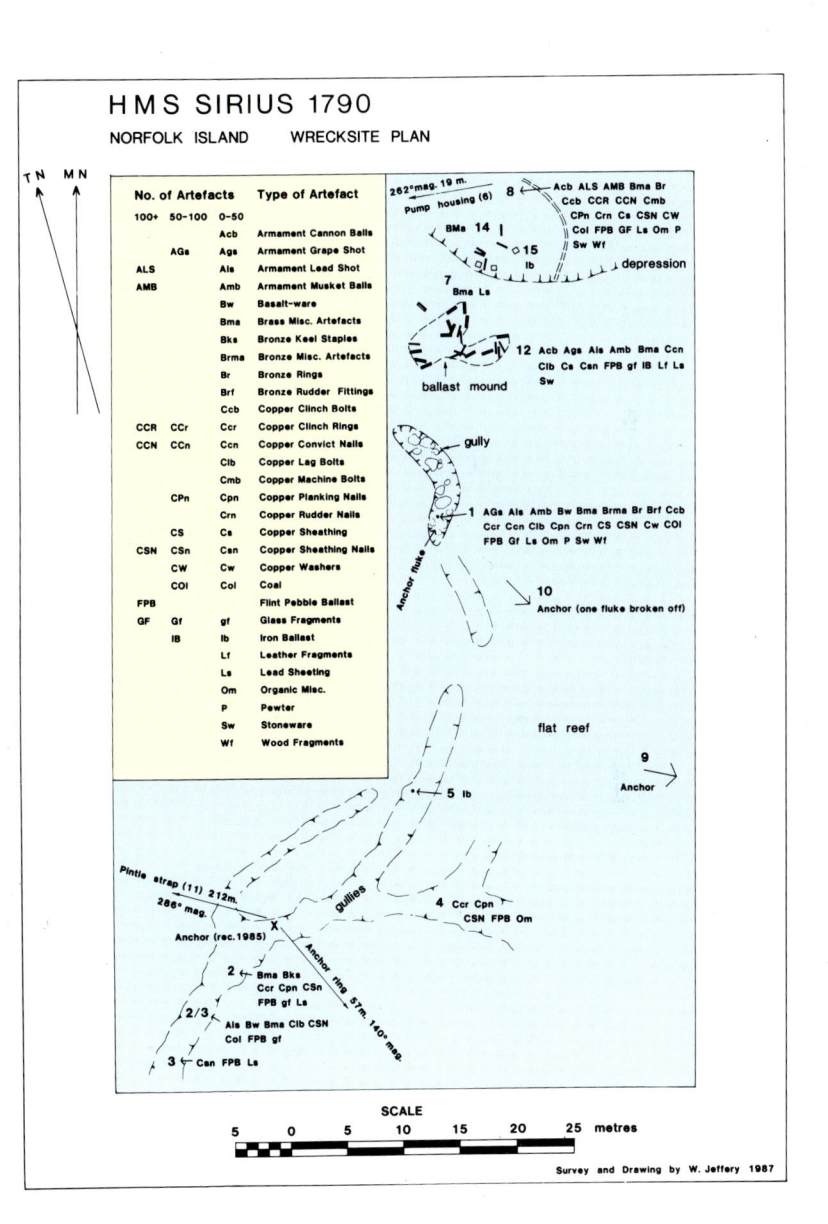

ARCHAEOLOGY

HMS SIRIUS 1790
NORFOLK ISLAND WRECKSITE PLAN

No. of Artefacts			Type of Artefact	
100+	50-100	0-50		
		Acb	Armament Cannon Balls
	AGs	Ags	Armament Grape Shot
ALS		Als	Armament Lead Shot
AMB		Amb	Armament Musket Balls
		Bw	Basalt-ware
		Bma	Brass Misc. Artefacts
		Bks	Bronze Keel Staples
		Brma	Bronze Misc. Artefacts
		Br	Bronze Rings
		Brf	Bronze Rudder Fittings
		Ccb	Copper Clinch Bolts
CCR	CCr	Ccr	Copper Clinch Rings
CCN	CCn	Ccn	Copper Convict Nails
		Clb	Copper Lag Bolts
		Cmb	Copper Machine Bolts
	CPn	Cpn	Copper Planking Nails
		Crn	Copper Rudder Nails
	CS	Cs	Copper Sheathing
CSN	CSn	Csn	Copper Sheathing Nails
	CW	Cw	Copper Washers
	COl	Col	Coal
FPB			Flint Pebble Ballast
GF		Gf	Glass Fragments
	IB	Ib	Iron Ballast
		Lf	Leather Fragments
		Ls	Lead Sheeting
		Om	Organic Misc.
		P	Pewter
		Sw	Stoneware
		Wf	Wood Fragments

SCALE 5 0 5 10 15 20 25 metres

Survey and Drawing by W. Jeffery 1987

surveying technique that requires tape measures and is based on trigonometry. Paul Clark linked the underwater survey with control stations on land, using a theodolite. Mark Staniforth led the magnetometer search for iron objects, carried out over a gridded area inside the lagoon. Expedition members conducted swimline searches over areas to the west of the Kingston pier as suggested by local divers. Five sites were investigated.

Site 1 is an area beneath and seaward of the zone affected by the swell. Charts from the 1790s and later indicate that this is where the ship struck and the wreck remained. Norfolk Island divers raised one anchor from this area in 1973, and divers consulted by expedition members universally assumed that this was the place where the *Sirius* finally broke up. Inspection of the site by *Sirius* Project members in 1983 led to a questioning of this assumption. The material observed – one complete anchor, two broken anchors, a small scattering of gravel ballast, several bronze bearings, lead sheathing fragments, copper-sheathing tacks, wood-sheathing nails, false-keel staples – seemed to Henderson and other project members to be more consistent with a stranding than with a total wreck. At the shoreward extremity of Site 1 were sternpost fittings. Captain Hunter's journal states that the *Sirius* lay stranded on the outer edge of the reef for ten days before being swept further inshore:

> ... the iron ballast having dropt out of her bottom, she was lifted fairly round, and was thrown more than her own length near to the shore, and was, by this change in her position, almost out of reach of the break of the sea; that is, the surf, which before generally broke upon her, now broke outside...[16]

Contemporary accounts give some indication of what was lost on the outside reef. Lieutenant Bradley wrote that the small bower anchor was cut away shortly before the *Sirius* struck. Such an anchor would be expected some distance seaward of the stranding site material, and the anchor raised in 1973 indeed came from such a location. The ring remains on the seabed. A second complete large anchor was observed in 1983, lying towards the seaward end of Site 1. This would be the other bower anchor, mentioned by Captain Hunter as having been dropped when the *Sirius* first struck. Its seabed location then may represent the position of the *Sirius*' bows during the first days on the reef. The vessel struck stern first, so the rudder would inevitably have been unshipped, to be swept, semi-submerged, away with the tide. After the vessel struck, Captain Hunter had the masts cut away to reduce the stress on the hull. One of Lieutenant Bradley's drawings indicates that the masts drifted ashore.

Two carronades fell overboard when the masts were cut down. One of these was observed in 1983, lying directly beneath the bower anchor, but the other carronade has not yet been located. Two anchors, each with a broken shank and a broken arm, lie further inshore on Site 1. Henderson interprets these broken anchors as the ballast, referred to by Hunter as having fallen out of the bottom of the *Sirius* prior to the hull being swept further inshore. Several iron ballast blocks lie close by. The palm of an anchor at the shoreward end of Site 1 is probably one of the two blasted from the anchor raised in 1905.

Site 2, lying immediately shoreward of Site 1, and including the shallow gully running along the outer perimeter of the high reef, proved in 1983 and 1985 to be the most difficult site for *Sirius* Project expedition members to investigate. The few items observed there in those years – case bottle fragments, stoneware fragments, lead sheathing, a musket ball, and several copper fastening bolts – were seen as being more consistent with the vessel's final breaking-up location than was the outer reef zone. However, the sea conditions did not at that time allow close investigation of Site 2.

Site 3. Expedition members could examine at leisure the high reef platform to the east of Kingston pier. During low tide the flat reef area partially dries. The iron work observed on that site is clearly from the 255-ton, three-masted auxiliary schooner *Renaki*, wrecked there in June 1943. Photographs show the *Renaki* high and dry on the reef platform, with residents commencing the task of salvaging what was useful. A stone causeway, running out from the shore to the high reef, has more obscure origins. The earliest known reference to it is on a 1904 chart. However, it seems probable that when Captain Hunter's men hauled the *Sirius'* guns ashore with their carriages in 1791, Hunter prepared a roadway of some kind first. Otherwise the gun-carriages, with their small wheels, could not have been rolled forwards. Convicts are known to have quarried stone from the high reef for the construction of buildings associated with their prison, but there appears to be no account of how they transported the stone ashore. Local residents report having found copper sheathing tacks along the shore after heavy storms, but generally Site 3 appeared to offer little archaeological potential.

Site 4. The *Sirius* Project investigated the Slaughter Bay lagoon on the premise that material from the *Sirius* would have been washed or carried in that direction, and that some would have remained there. Being calm and shallow, the site was well suited to a seabed search. It was thought that the sand bottom might have offered a superior preservation medium to that of Site 3. However, the seabed in the gridded area proved to consist of a thin layer of sand, generally less than 20 centimetres, over a flat bed of irregular 5 to 20-centimetre pieces of coralline debris which interlocked to form an almost impenetrable layer of unknown depth. This makes it unlikely that any substantial material would have been buried in much of the area to the extent necessary for preservation. One rectangular iron ballast pig was located. Despite its weight of over 50 kilograms, it had not buried itself in the layer of coralline debris. There was no evidence, such as iron or copper fastenings, to indicate that this piece had drifted to the middle of the lagoon supported by structure from the *Sirius*. Nor does it seem likely that a boat carrying the piece ashore from the reef would have capsized there. Given its weight, the piece would have been suitable as a small-boat mooring, and that may well have been the reason for its location in the lagoon.

Site 4 did not appear to have much potential. Any further magnetometer work, it seemed, would best be conducted in the area closest to the high reef, where the sand layer appears to be deeper.

Site 5 is an area west of Kingston pier that contains wreckage. Local divers had raised material from this site, including a spectacle plate – part of a jury steering system – marked *BERWICK*. The *Sirius* project examined the site with a view to identification of other material from the *Sirius*. It quickly became clear that material from several shipwrecks, as well as modern rubbish thrown from Kingston pier, had collected in the area. The vast bulk of the wreckage was consistent with the whaler *Mary Hamilton,* run ashore there in 1873.

Metallurgical analysis of material from this site would be necessary to give an indication of how much *Sirius* material was deposited there, but the distance from the principal deposit makes it unlikely that much would be found. It is most likely that the rudder, or the

A treatment tank, custom built for the bower anchor by staff at the Norfolk Island Administrative Works Depot. Photograph by Jon Carpenter, 1986.
AUSTRALIAN BICENTENNIAL AUTHORITY

after part of it, drifted there in 1790. If so, other fittings from the rudder are likely to have been deposited in the same place.

In March 1986 Jon Carpenter, a conservator from the Western Australian Museum's Department of Materials Conservation and Restoration, visited Norfolk Island to help islanders to prepare the anchor and carronade, raised in 1985, for treatment by electrolytic reduction.[17] Objects were treated on Norfolk Island because of a desire by the community, shared by the *Sirius* Project, that Norfolk Island maintain some control of the collection. The arrangement whereby the objects are treated by Norfolk Island people with the advice and assistance the Western Australian Museum's conservators is working well.

In 1987, Graeme Henderson led another twelve-person expedition to Norfolk Island for three weeks of work on the *Sirius* site. The Australian Bicentennial Authority continued to fund the *Sirius* Project and assumed a more participatory administrative role. Senior project officer Mary Smith accompanied the expedition as the authority's representative. Other new faces on the project were Bill Jeffery, an archaeologist from the South Australian Department of Environment and Planning, Heritage Conservation Branch, Geoff Kimpton, in charge of equipment, from the Western Australian Maritime Museum, Sharon Towns, conservator with the Museums Association of Australia, New South Wales Branch, and Maree Edmiston, an artist, from Queensland. The intention was to complete the survey in Sites 1 to 4, and to make a last attempt to locate the final resting position of the wreck, although no one on the project expected that much new evidence would be found, given the generally flat reef structure and the constant white-water conditions.

Excellent sea conditions made diving possible on seven of the nineteen days the team spent on the island. During that time the survey work on Site 1 was completed, and the opportunity taken to explore the potential of Site 2. Sites 3 and 4 were not of high priority; their easy accessibility from the land to early salvagers, and the obvious heavy contamination of the area with material from several periods, limited their archaeological potential. In the event, no attention was given to them.

The breaking waves caused masses of white bubbles which extended to the seabed, preventing any clear view of Site 2. Divers only gradually became aware of the volume of material below the bubble screen. It was not until the eleventh day of the expedition that the presence of a mound of dozens of iron ballast blocks was realised. Geoff Kimpton, a veteran surf diver, saw the first indications in that area. Divers found material that related not just to the construction of the vessel, but also to its fitting out, manning and provisioning. It became apparent that this was where the *Sirius* finally broke up, and that a very substantial quantity of material still lies on the site.

Soon after the 1987 field season, the Australian Bicentennial Authority arranged for Henderson to spend two weeks examining archival sources at the Public Record Office and the National Maritime Museum in London. These libraries contain the government records of the British navy and the departments that organised the First Fleet. Henderson's work concentrated on records about the building and fitting out of the *Sirius* – royal dockyard letterbooks, Admiralty correspondence, Navy Office letters, ships' muster books, captains' and masters' logbooks, and Ordnance Office correspondence. Myra Stanbury followed up with research in British museums, aimed at identifying the objects found on the *Sirius* wreck site.

The result of the field and archival investigations has been a new awareness among *Sirius* Project members of a broader research potential for the *Sirius* site. The fieldwork, in locating the principal archaeological deposit, has opened the way to a more comprehensive testing of the Muckelroy model of the relationship between environment and site condition. Closer examination of the ballast mound could even reveal some minor structural remains. The archival investigations have produced a wealth of information, leading to an altogether different interpretation of the building, fitting out and suitability of the *Sirius*. *Sirius* Project members have arranged a testing of the hypothesis 'that the chronological process of wrecking and ship breakup can be elucidated by the examination of the spatial patterning of artefact remains'. This hypothesis is being examined in an honours dissertation by student Gaye Nayton at the Centre for Prehistory, University of Western Australia.

The most important historical question now posed relates to the *Sirius*' condition when she commenced the First Fleet voyage, and her suitability for such a voyage. Consider the broader issue. Was the transporting of convicts to Australia intended merely as a stopgap measure to rid Britain of the nuisance of overcrowded prison hulks, or was it part of a considered long-term strategy, to develop a new empire in the Antipodes? In the bicentennial year this is one of the most pertinent questions relating to our national identity being addressed by historians. To find the answer to this question it is necessary to look both at what was said and what was done in preparing for the Botany Bay settlement. Historian Alan Frost put it this way:

> No one has yet described adequately the mounting of the First Fleet. The relevant documents in Historical Records of New South Wales are only a small portion of those extant... A comprehensive description of this mounting would bury the myths that the Pitt administration were generally indolent in assembling the Fleet, that they equipped the colonising party poorly, and that these features reflect their common disregard of the convicts' welfare.[18]

Frost sees what documentary evidence has been explored as supporting his view of a well-prepared fleet:

> According to Teer the transports were 'Completely fitted', with their 'Provisions and accommodations' being 'better than any [other] set of transports I have ever had any directions in.'[19]

In the archaeological remains and the archival records specifically relating to the *Sirius* we have the opportunity to test Frost's assumption that there was a well-orchestrated colonisation plan. What is required is an analysis of the remains of the ship and its fittings in the light of historical knowledge of shipbuilding, ship maintenance and fitting out practices in Britain's navy in the late eighteenth century. The archival research in London has already contributed substantially to this analysis, indicating that the *Sirius* was the appropriate choice for a government intending to establish a colony in New South Wales.

Another historical question briefly considered at the commencement of the *Sirius* Project was that of the contrast in origins between the 'East Indiaman'-built *Sirius* and other vessels sent out to the Pacific in the late eighteenth century, such as the collier-built *Endeavour* and *Resolution*, and the navy transports *Supply* and *Bounty*. The new interpretation of the *Berwick* as being of Baltic-trader build changes all that. We are now looking at a weatherly, roomy, cost-efficient ship of Baltic tradition.

Professor Ralph Davis, who in his standard work, *The Rise of the English Shipping Industry*, sees great significance in the Dutch flyboat's hull form and manning efficiency for Baltic traders, then colliers and eventually even the Virginia traders, all of which were influenced by the flyboat's economical hull shape, writes:

> East India ships were alone in maintaining very heavy manning. It is to be hoped that nautical archaeologists will one day investigate these matters [relating to merchant vessel hull form]...[20]

It would seem that Britain, in choosing a Baltic trader and navy transport rather than an East Indiaman, was wisely opting for roominess and weatherliness rather than a large, strongly built, well furnished and handsomely decorated, but inappropriate vessel.

CHAPTER 9
Relics from the *Sirius*

Although a definitive spatial analysis of the *Sirius* artefacts has yet to be completed, the 1987 plan of the wreck site gives some idea of the relative abundance and clustering of artefacts in particular areas of the main site, Site 1. Even at this preliminary stage, a pattern of distribution is emerging that is consistent with the historical account of the *Sirius* being thrown stern first upon the reef.

Working from south to north, that is, from the outer reef inshore, Areas 3 to 2 produced predominantly flint pebble ballast, a variety of copper alloy fastenings, a small amount of lead shot and a few glass and ceramic fragments. More significant were a number of bronze keel staples. Area 4 produced copper alloy fastenings and a small amount of organic material, while Area 5 contained an iron ballast block.

Further north in Area 1, a more varied assemblage of artefacts had been deposited in the gully: an assortment of armament including a moderate quantity of grape shot, lead shot and musket balls; bronze pintles and gudgeons which would have held the rudder in place, along with rudder nails and lag bolts. There were bronze coaks, long, clinched copper keel bolts and more ships' fastenings, a quantity of coal, lead sheeting, and yet more flint pebble ballast. Among a diver's collection of ballast was a stone unlike the others, an edge-ground stone hatchet head of Aboriginal origin.

The other significant discoveries in this area were a brass sextant, a pantograph, and parts of navigation dividers. In addition there was a small brass button, fragments of glass containers and utilitarian salt-glazed stoneware jars. A few engine-turned basaltware fragments could only have come from a more elaborate and expensive urn or vase, such as those being made by Josiah Wedgewood at the time the *Sirius* sailed from England.

Divers found a substantial mound of iron ballast at Area 12, as well as a few cannon balls and the odd one or two musket balls and grape shot. By far the most interesting item recovered from this area was a beautifully engraved brass fire-grate leg of Neoclassical style, a form

A concretion containing washers, screws and nails. Photograph by Pat Baker, 1987.
AUSTRALIAN BICENTENNIAL AUTHORITY

which gradually replaced the serpentine Rococo designs from the 1760s.[1] A beaded section of the grate was found close by, along with an oval patera wall fitting or cloak pin, also of Neoclassical design. At Area 7, a brass shoulder-belt plate from the uniform of an officer of the Royal Marines was located, and another similar one was found in Area 8.

Situated in a depression, Area 8 yielded a large and varied assemblage of artefacts. About 50 per cent of the cannon balls recovered during the expedition came from this region, 96 per cent of the musket balls and 92 per cent of the lead shot. Associated finds were a brass wrist escutcheon and ramrod pipes from Land Pattern muskets, along with two gunflints; brass and pewter uniform buttons, one decorated with an anchor; a brass cloak pin with a classical urn design; brass taps and spigots; more fragments of navigational instruments; assorted glassware and flat window glass fragments; small pieces of decorated blue and white porcelain; wood and other organic material.

The temporary field conservation laboratory, in a government boatshed on Norfolk Island. Photograph by Pat Baker, 1987.
AUSTRALIAN BICENTENNIAL AUTHORITY.

Items probably being carried as cargo or stores were predominant in Area 8: assorted sizes of forged, rose-headed copper nails and washers, and, at least three sizes of clinch rings, each clearly stamped with a broad arrow. Here too, were numerous sheathing and planking nails, machine bolts, rudder nails, bronze coaks and copper sheathing.

RELICS RELATING TO THE STRUCTURE AND FITTINGS

Various fastenings have been recovered from the *Sirius* wreck site which relate to the structural components the ship's **hull**, but very little has been found which represents the **bow** of the vessel except a bronze 'horse plate'. Shaped like a horseshoe, this was used at the front of the keel to fasten together the keel, stem and gripe. It was raised prior to the *Sirius* Project's investigations.

Several types of fastenings may be associated with the **keel** or main backbone of the ship. Only two iron bolts have been found, which may indicate that almost all the remaining iron was replaced with copper during the Sydney Cove refit. It may also reflect the inferior survival characteristics of ferrous material on a wave-swept site. There has been to date only limited investigation of Site 2 where keel bolts might be expected to be found.

The few bronze and copper keel staples, located primarily in Area 2, would have fastened the false keel to the main keel. The latter was made of several lengths of timber fitted together by means of scarph joints, secured with clinch bolts. Holding the keel, floor timbers and keelson together were long clinch bolts, sometimes referred to as drift or through bolts.[2] Besides those actually used in the construction of the vessel, there were also spare copper bolts, carried in the after hold during the First Fleet voyage. A small number of long clinch bolts, ranging from 420 millimetres (16.5 inches) to 585 millimetres (23 inches) in length and 32 millimetres (1.25 inches) to 35 millimetres (1.37 inches) in diameter, were found in Area 1. All were of copper and had broad arrows, signifying that they were Royal Navy issue, stamped on the shafts and clinch rings.[3] One copper alloy forelock bolt was also found in Area 1 and would have been used as a hull fastening. The metallurgical analysis of a copper rod or bar from the *Sirius* identified it as an impure tough-pitch copper probably fabricated from an ingot by cold hammering.[4]

Copper alloy forged planking nails, of up to 88 millimetres (3.5 inches) in length, were found in Areas 1, 2, 4 and 8, the majority being from Area 8. Likewise, copper alloy sheathing nails, some for the purpose of driving through wood sheathing planks and some for driving through copper sheets, together with copper sheathing fragments, were found in Areas 1, 2, 2–3, 4, 8, and 12, the main concentrations being in Areas 1 and 8. A metallurgical analysis of some sheathing nails from the *Sirius* carried out in 1983 found them to be cast from arsenical tin bronze of a composition that does not correspond closely to any common modern alloy.[5]

While both the copper bar and nails were of poor metallurgical quality, reflecting the level of technology in the mid-eighteenth century, they had performed their function satisfactorily. The bar was strong enough for a bolt, and the nails had good corrosion resistance.[6]

In Areas 2 and 8 one or two square-shank 'brass' spikes were located, the broad arrow stamped on the shafts. Their metallugical composition has not yet been examined, though a 'brass' bolt

Chisel-pointed copper planking nails. Photograph by Pat Baker, 1987.
AUSTRALIAN BICENTENNIAL AUTHORITY

recovered from Site 5 in 1985 was found to be a low tin bronze.[7] Wood attached to this bolt was identified as chestnut (*Castanae* species), probably *Castanae sativa* or European chestnut.[8] Wild chestnut timber was considered by some shipbuilders to be as good as oak[9] and was used in the framing of some ships.[10]

A number of fittings were recovered which relate to the **stern** of the ship, in particular the sternpost and the rudder. A system of gudgeons and pintles allowed the rudder to be hinged against the sternpost: the pintles, fastened to the rudder, have a downward projecting pin which slots into a hole in the gudgeons, fastened to the sternpost and stern planking. The rudder was approximately the same thickness as the sternpost and tapered gradually as it rose from the level of the keel to the waterline. From there, it was tapered by means of a series of steps to produce an almost square head able to take the tiller.[11]

One complete and two broken gudgeons, a pintle minus its pin, two broken pins, and two straps were recovered from Site 1 prior to the *Sirius* Project. Their association with the *Sirius* was confirmed by metallurgical and chemical analysis.[12] In 1987 three more pintle or gudgeon straps were recovered, two from Site 1 and one from Area 11 at the end of the Kingston pier, 212 metres northwest of the anchor recovered from Site 1 in 1985. One strap from Site 1 was in excellent condition and had some fastenings in situ. This indicated that copper alloy rudder nails, alternating with copper alloy lag bolts or screws, were used to fix the gudgeons and pintles to the sternpost and rudder. Both types of fastenings were concentrated in Areas 1 and 8.

The *Berwick* had five sets of pintles and gudgeons. To date, the collection of relics recovered by the *Sirius* Project and Norfolk Islanders contains at least three, if not parts of all five gudgeons, although only one pintle and three pintle pins have been definitely identified.

The rudder was an essential part of the steering system of the ship. As a precaution against accidental loss or lifting of the pintles from the gudgeons, strong ropes or rudder pendants were rigged and shackled to the eyes of a bronze spectacle plate fastened to the trailing edge of the rudder at a point just above the waterline, above the fourth pintle on the *Berwick*. The ropes led inboard on each side of the ship through shackles secured to the hull and thence to manned tackles inboard. In the event of the tiller breaking or the upper part of the rudder being damaged in action, this system of ropes could be used to keep the rudder under control.[13]

A bronze spectacle plate, now in the care of Kerry Coop, was recovered by Norfolk Island diver Mike Simpson from Site 5, to the west of the Kingston pier, some years prior to the *Sirius* Project. Despite the distance from the main wreck site, it is undoubtedly from the *Sirius*. The name BERWICK is cast into the band and its metallurgical composition corresponds with the bronze pintles and gudgeons recovered from the main wreck site. A bronze shackle and two chain links discovered by Peter Ely of Norfolk Island on the main wreck site, would have been associated with the rigging of the rudder pendants. One of the links is capable of being opened, thus providing a facility for rigging the ropes or altering the length of the chains as required.

During the 1786 refit, moulds were taken of the *Sirius*' rudder and fittings, in case spares should be required. It is certain, given that the copper sheathing was never removed, that the vessel had carried the same spectacle plate since her construction in 1780–81. A similar piece found on the wreck of HMS *Pandora*, built for the navy, was marked with broad arrows.

In the 1780s rudder fittings were often badly made:

> Upon our late survey of Mr Forbes' metal braces and pintles for ships of the several rates building and repairing, we have discovered a number of them vary from 4 to 6 hundredweight [203.2 to 304.8 kg] the set which not only subjects them to be unnecessarily heavy but very expensive, which Mr Forbes attributes entirely to the moulds being badly made.[14]

When the *Supply* was taken on for the First Fleet voyage her rudder fittings were checked for imperfections and corrosion:

> …we have surveyed the braces and pintles purchased by Mr Collins and put on the *Supply* Transport in April 1785 in this dock, and find them in a perfect state…[15]

Purpose-built Royal Navy ships, other than small vessels, were generally fitted with two **pump systems**: the main chain or yard pumps and the common or elm-tree suction pumps. The former were for clearing the bilges and dealing with leakages and the latter were used for supplying fresh salt water for cleaning the decks or for firefighting. The elm-tree pumps consisted of an upper and lower barrel of elm, with a central working barrel of mixed metal or bronze. They took in water via a small pipe leading through the side of the ship, just beneath the waterline, and generally led to the upper deck, rather than the gun deck.[16] The pumps were situated port and starboard of the middle line, amidships, adjacent to the main pumps, that is, either side of the mainmast.

Pieces of lead sheet and piping scattered through Sites 1 and 2 are possibly evidence of plumbing arrangements. Several bronze coaks may also be associated with the pump mechanisms. In Areas 1 and 6, two sections of a bronze pump barrel with a bore measuring 156.5 millimetres were found. A similar piece had been found on the site prior to the *Sirius* Project's investigations. The *Pandora* site, too, has yielded a bronze pump barrel section with a 170-millimetre bore. The 1781 draught of the *Berwick* indicates that she was fitted with common pumps as her main pumps. The common pump consisted of a long wooden tube, whose lower end rested upon the ship's bottom, between the timbers, in the well. It would appear that the lower bore chamber was frequently made of bronze, with a nozzle attachment of lead.

During her 1786 refit the *Sirius* had her well enlarged and her old pumps replaced with four new ones. Partners (strengthening planks) were fitted round the hand pumps. It is likely that the *Sirius* then had two pump systems: main chain pumps together with main common pumps and small hand-operated common pumps.

It was traditional for the officers of the ship to have their quarters in the stern. This was considered the most comfortable part of the ship and allowed easy access to the steering mechanisms. Apartments were luxurious compared to those of the common seamen, and the captain's cabin usually gave him access to the stern gallery. A number of artefacts recovered from Areas 8 and 12 give us some idea of the type of cabin furnishings and fittings likely to have been in the **captain's or officers' quarters.**

Numerous flat glass fragments, particularly in Area 8, would most likely have come from the windows of the stern galleries. Stone-ground glass was available at Deptford when the *Berwick* was being built. Curtains would probably have been used across the windows or doorways to block out light and draughts, ties being used to secure them in an open position. An oval brass wall fitting with a patera design may well have served as a curtain tie-back. A small iron screw at the base of the pedestal has corroded away but would have allowed the fitting to be screwed into the wooden cabin wall. It could just as well function as a cloak pin for hanging hats or other items of apparel, or even as a decorative support for a mirror.[17]

A second brass furniture fitting represents a classical urn surrounded by an oval wreath of laurel leaves. Again, the attachment on the reverse has corroded away, but it is likely to have been a screw, enabling the fitting to be fastened as a mount to a piece of furniture or to the wall, as in the previous instance. Both designs, which could be either stamped or cast, appear with regularity in late eighteenth-century catalogues of brass furniture fittings and conform to the Neoclassical patterns of the period.[18] Brass founders in London and, more especially, Birmingham, were producing large quantities of furniture fittings and mounts for the export market, particularly for North America. The fittings were often poorly finished and were generally polished and lacquered rather than gilded.

Naval warships during most of the eighteenth century had no regular system of heating since the danger of combustion prevented the lighting of fires on decks. Officers sometimes had small stoves fitted in their cabins or in the wardroom. During his voyage to Cape of Good Hope late in 1788 Captain Hunter wrote:

...the thermometer was down to 42 degrees in the cabin, where we sometimes had a fire... [19]

In 1783 movable iron stoves were issued, at the rate of one for each deck, to create an airflow intended to prevent disease and the decay of timbers as well as discomfort to the crew.[20] Brodie's airing stoves were still being issued at the rate of two per 20-gun ship in 1786, when the *Sirius* was being fitted out for her long voyage.[21]

A finely engraved brass fire-grate leg along with a beaded skirt section were both recovered from Area 12. The ornate engraving suggests that these are from a stove in the officers' quarters, if not from the captain's cabin itself. The straight lines of the leg are typical of the Neoclassical style of furniture. The most popular Neoclassical motifs were all drawn from Roman sources and included

Engraved brass fire-grate leg (left). Terry Arnott examines the fire-grate leg. Photographs by Pat Baker, 1987.
AUSTRALIAN BICENTENNIAL AUTHORITY

round or oval paterae, strings of husks or bell flowers, urns, griffins and winged sphinxes. Examples of some of these decorative devices may be seen on three sides of the brass leg. The fourth side, which would not have been visible when the grate was in use, is not decorated and bears rough filing or casting marks only.

In the top of the leg is a threaded hole into which a finial would have been screwed, completing this extremely handsome piece of craftsmanship.[22] A plain brass strip, beaded along each edge, would probably have formed the skirt of the grate, while the main fire-box of the stove would have been made of heavy cast iron, to reflect heat. Probably it would have been cast with similar motifs to those on the leg. The *Pandora* site has yielded a cabin stove, complete with its smoke funnel. A brass leg and finial from the *Pandora* are also engraved with Neoclassical motifs.

When away at sea for long periods, regular officers often took certain of their own household possessions with them to furnish their cabins during spells in ports of call. Knowing they were likely to be spending a considerable period of time away from England, with or without the prospect of setting up a temporary home in New South Wales, it is hardly surprising that the remains of objects unlikely to have been standard navy issue have been found on the *Sirius* wreck site.

Among the few identifiable glass and ceramic fragments found were pieces of a lead glass decanter stopper and blue and white porcelain exhibiting features of Spode's willow pattern. Especially notable, however, were a few fragments of black engine-turned basaltware. Staffordshire potters had been manufacturing black wares from the beginning of the eighteenth century, but it was Josiah Wedgewood who perfected the production of this fine black stoneware around 1768, adding to its general popularity both in England and overseas. Although Wedgewood produced items of domestic utility, his first strictly ornamental wares were developed using this medium. The vessels were often cast and additional decoration formed on the engine-turning lathe. Designs often included the urns and vases of Neoclassical style, much like the urn on the brass furniture mount.[23] Wedgewood was certainly a well-known and influential figure in the late eighteenth century and made an elegant medallion for Arthur Phillip in about 1789 from New South Wales clay symbolising 'Hope encouraging Art and Labour, under the influence of Peace, to pursue the employments necessary to give security and happiness to an infant settlement'.[24]

The distribution of weight in a sailing ship could decisively affect the trim, and therefore the sailing quality of the vessel. The master, responsible to the captain for the technical aspects of sailing the ship, was in charge of the **stowage of ballast,** cargo and other materials in the hold.

Iron ballast was laid down first, fore and aft in the main hold, followed by shingle. Iron ballast blocks, weighing approximately 105 kilograms (232 pounds) each, have been recovered from the *Sirius* wreck site. In 1782, one-hundredweight (50.8-kilogram) blocks were described as small pieces.[25] Several sizes have been observed on the ballast mound on the site. The blocks recovered are stamped with the broad arrow mark and have a hole at each end where they would have been chained together to prevent any movement as the ship pitched and tossed. The Carron Company and Messrs Barnes Hoddington were among British companies making iron ballast, at a little under £8 per ton, in the 1780s.

The washed and screened shingle ballast was laid on top of the iron ballast and formed a bed into which the casks of provisions could sink. The shingle ballast from the *Sirius* consisted of flint pebbles. They are typical of the stones found in the River Thames, and for each ton (1.02 tonnes) taken on board, British ships were bound to pay the corporation of the Trinity-house 1s 3d.[26] The actual amount of ballast for a particular ship was usually settled by her designer, and this was enforced by the orders of the Navy Board. A ship of 400 tons, carrying twenty guns, could be expected to carry approximately 50 tons (51 tonnes) of iron and 60 tons (61.2 tonnes) of shingle ballast. The *Sirius* was expected to carry 80 tons (81.6 tonnes) of iron ballast.

Coal, found in various places on the site, would also have contributed to the ballast, likewise the casks of water and victuals and items being carried as stores or cargo.[27] Brass keg taps and spigots were found in Areas 1 and 8 along with several fragments of square-sided case or spirits bottles and dark green wine bottles. Several brown salt-glazed stoneware sherds in these areas have clearly come from wide-mouth jars commonly used to store drugs or provisions. Similar jars found on the *Pandora* site contained a variety of medicinal compounds. By far the greatest number of cargo items, however, was in Area 8. Here, quantities of unused copper clinch rings, various sizes of rose-headed forged copper nails[28] and copper washers were concentrated. There was also a small number of machine bolts. The function of these is not yet clear, though fastenings of this kind are generally used to fasten iron fittings to wood.

As regards relics of the **rigging** of the *Sirius*, several bronze coaks or bushes have been found on the wreck site but it is doubtful that they are from pulley block sheaves since they have no flanges for rivetting them in place. Blocks of more than 10 inches (25.4 centimetres) being supplied to the navy in 1787 were said to be:

> Plank Coaked Shivers with Brass Plates rivetted at the centre to wear on turned iron pins and all under 8 ins to be wood pinned as usual.[29]

RELICS RELATING TO THE CREW AND PASSENGERS

Probably the most interesting objects raised from Area 1 were a brass sextant, a pantograph and several sections of brass navigation dividers. In preparing for the voyage to Botany Bay, both **Captain Arthur Phillip** and **Lieutenant William Dawes** of the Royal Marines requested loans of navigation and astronomical instruments from the Board of Longitude in London. Dawes was obviously a keen and capable astronomer as Dr. Nevil Maskelyne, the Astronomer Royal, had little hesitation in recommending to the board that he be allowed to borrow instruments and books to enable him to make nautical and astronomical observations during and after his passage to Botany Bay on the *Sirius*.[30] The board agreed on the condition that Captain Phillip be charged with the responsibility for their care and preservation, which Phillip agreed to.[31] In addition, Phillip himself asked the board for the loan of a 'Timekeeper'.

In November 1786, Larcum Kendall's Marine Timekeeper K1 was lent to Captain Arthur Phillip. This chronometer had been used by Captain Cook on his second voyage (1772–1775) in HMS *Resolution* and had maintained excellent time.[32] Used again on Cook's third voyage (1776–1780), the chronometer stopped shortly after Cook died off Kamchatka.[33] It was found to have dirt in the mechanism and a broken pendulum spring and attempts to clean and repair it were unsuccessful. At the end of the voyage K1 was returned to its maker for repair and subsequently returned to Greenwich in 1786.

Dawes took the watch to the Royal Naval Academy at Portsmouth for rating in December 1786 but had it returned to Greenwich for further adjustment as it was not performing satisfactorily.[34] After a final check at the academy a few days prior to the *Sirius*' departure, the Kendall K1 chronometer was taken on board. Phillip ordered that it be wound daily at noon in the presence of **Captain Hunter,** Lieutenant Dawes or himself. To further ensure that the timepiece would not be allowed to run down, the marine duty officer and duty sentry were to be present when the clock was wound in the captain's cabin.[35] Dawes was also given the responsibility of using the chronometer to calculate the ship's longitude.

At Rio de Janeiro when the rate of the clock was checked[36] Captain Hunter commented that it had been very regular. When

The Harrison No. 4 (left) and the Kendall No. 1 Timekeepers.
NATIONAL MARITIME MUSEUM, GREENWICH

Phillip transferred to the *Supply*, he took Dawes and K1 with him, returning the chronometer to the *Sirius* when it arrived in Botany Bay. The valuable timepiece was on board when the *Sirius* was wrecked at Norfolk Island. Dawes must have felt great relief in being able to write to Nevil Maskelyne on 16 April 1790 that: 'In consequence of the loss of the *Sirius* the Timekeeper is now in the *Supply*. It did not receive the slightest injury...'[37] The famous chronometer may be seen today at the Old Royal Observatory, Greenwich.

Other instruments and books which would have been on board the *Sirius*, loaned to Dawes and acknowledged by Phillip on 16 May 1787, were as follows: '1 N.M. An Astronomical Clock, 2 N.M. The wooden stand of Do. composed of pieces morticed together, The journeyman clock, The alarm clock, Two thermometers, An astronomical quadrant by Bird, An old Hadley's sextant by Ramsden about 14 or 15 inches radius, A divided object glass micrometer for the 3½ feet telescope, A wooden quadrant with its telescope, applied to the 3½ feet telescope, A 3½ feet achromatic telescope with its stand and 2 micrometers with oblique wires [by Dolland], A Graham's Micrometer, A declination semicircle & mahogany stand to use with the night telescope, Kendall's first time keeper, The nautical almanac from 1787 to 1792 and Tables requisite to be used with the nautical almanac.'[38]

Other books and instruments received by Dawes included: 'Gardiner's Logarithms reprinted at Avignon's, Sherwin's Logarithms, Hadley's Tables; The Nautical Almanac from 1787 to 1792 £63 inclusive, The Requisite Tables, A New 10 inch Sextant by Ramsden, A Pocket Watch with a second hand and ruby Palletts.'[39]

The board had agreed to purchase the new improved 10-inch Ramsden sextant for Dawes to use on the expedition on 3 February 1787.[40] He received this from Dr. Maskelyne, along with the pocket watch, on 8 February 1787.[41] The presence of ruby pallets is an indication that the watch may have been the work of London watchmaker John Ellicott or his son Edward, noted for jewelled mechanisms at this time.[42] A pocket watch similar to the one Dawes would have been given, made by J. & J. Jackson, was recovered from the *Pandora*.[43]

In November 1791, Phillip wrote to the Board of Longitude notifying them that the astronomical instruments salvaged from the *Sirius* by Lieutenant Dawes were being returned in HMS *Gorgon* and that the timekeeper had been placed in the care of Lieutenant Lidgbird Ball of the *Supply*.[44] From the receipt of instruments by John Crawford, master of the *Gorgon*, it is clear that Dawes did a remarkable job in salvaging almost all of the instruments on loan.[45] No mention is made of the 10-inch Ramsden sextant or the pocket watch, but since these had been specifically assigned to Dawes he would undoubtedly have ensured their retrieval, especially since the old sextant by Ramsden was salvaged.

Sextants had been in use since the early eighteenth century and were exclusively used in observations at sea. They were far more accurate than quadrants, and extended the range of angular readings from 90 to 120 degrees. Their name refers to the arc of the instrument, which occupies a sixth of a circle – 60 degrees – and not to the angle that can be measured. By measuring the angular distance between the moon and the sun, or a fixed star, navigators were able to determine the longitude of their position. The first sextants were

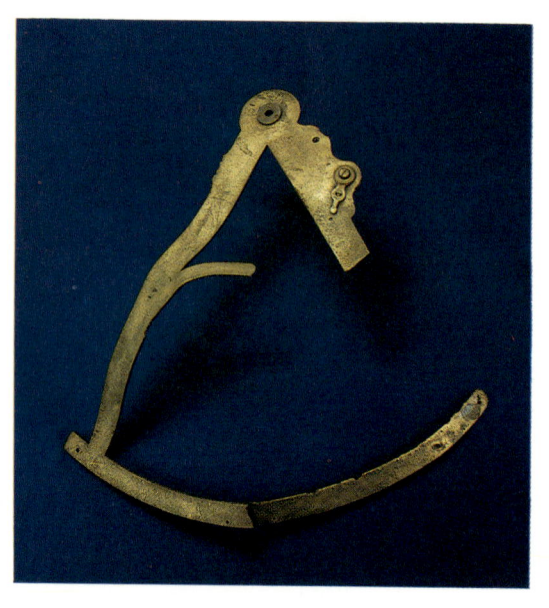

Reverse side of the sextant after conservation treatment. Photograph by Pat Baker, 1987.
AUSTRALIAN BICENTENNIAL AUTHORITY

large, with radii of about 20 inches, and correspondingly heavy. Smaller instruments became possible with improved techniques of accurate scale division. One of the important steps in the development of the sextant was Jesse Ramsden's invention of a machine for engraving scales mechanically – his 'dividing engine' of 1771 – which enabled instruments of smaller radius to be supplied with accurate scales.

A sextant with a radius of 15 inches, recovered from the *Sirius* wreck site, was made by a London instrument maker, but unfortunately the name on the cross bar has been abraded and only the word 'London' in copperplate script remains. It is compatible with the period 1770–1780, but is one of the cheaper varieties of sextant available at that time. The scale is well divided and calibrated from zero to 125 degrees, each degree being further divided into two 30-minute parts, but the absence of a Board of Longitude scale stamp, that is, a foul anchor with the divider's initials on either side, makes it difficult to say whether the scale was engine-divided or not.[46] Clearly, it was not the most up-to-date instrument at the time the *Sirius* sailed: the smaller Ramsden sextant loaned to Dawes would have been far superior.

A number of small fittings were associated with the frame of the sextant, such as an adjusting screw, telescope, lens mount and so on. It became clear from the number of pieces found, however, that there was more than one sextant of this design on board the *Sirius*. Indeed, a similar frame section was recovered from the wreck site by Karl Davies of Norfolk Island before the *Sirius* Project began its work. Whether these instruments were standard navy issue or the personal equipment of one of the officers has yet to be determined.

The brass pantograph, discovered in the same gully as the sextant, is a kind of parallel link-motion instrument designed to copy maps, plans or other drawings to the same, a larger, or a smaller scale. These instruments were referred to in London instrument-makers' advertisements as 'Pentographas' or 'Pantographers, for reducing Drawings and Pictures of any Size, in the most complete Manner'.[47] The pantograph was invented in the early seventeenth century by the German astronomer Christoph Scheiner and improved in 1743 by the Parisian craftsman Claude Langlois.[48]

The device consists of four brass bars, jointed in pairs, one pair being twice the length of the other. Small castors of ivory support the instrument parallel to the paper, so that it can move freely over the paper in all directions. One long bar has a tracing point, and a short arm has a pen held by a sliding head that is set to the ratio required. To vary the pressure of the pen on the paper, the pen holder is loaded with small weights. A fine thread passing round the top of the instrument enables the draughtsman or cartographer to raise the pen from the paper while the tracing point is passed from one part of the original plan to another, thereby obviating false lines on the copy. On the other long bar is a pivot point in the form of a heavy brass disc or weight.

The pantograph arm from the *Sirius* bears no maker's name. It is graduated in the proportions of $1/2$, $5/11$, $2/5$, $1/3$, $1/5$, $1/6$, $1/7$, $1/8$, $1/9$, $1/10$, $1/11$, $1/12$. The letter 'B' engraved on the sliding frame and on the arm indicates that this would have been one of the short arms of the instrument, the pen-holding device having broken away from the sliding frame. The instrument has been precision made, small dots on the screw heads and sliding frame indicating the correct position for individual screws. Another section of the pantograph was recovered by Karl Davies and is displayed, along with other *Sirius* artefacts, in the *Bounty* Museum, Norfolk Island.

Long-distance sea voyages in the late eighteenth century put as much strain on the health of ships' crews and passengers as they did on the ships themselves. 'Sea diseases' were largely the consequence of poor nutrition and the inability to preserve foodstuffs by means other than salt. Considerable advances had been made to combat many of the common diseases, particularly those related to vitamin deficiencies, such as scurvy.

While fresh oranges, lemons and vegetables would help to keep scurvy at bay, ships travelling in tropical waters would be exposed to other kinds of infections – malaria, for example, or illnesses contracted from contaminated water supplies. Ships' medical officers thus had to equip themselves with a broad range of supplies to cater for any eventuality.

Salt-glazed stoneware jar fragments from Areas 1, 8 and 12 could be related to the provisions on board, but may well have been part of the **surgeon's** inventory. The jars were impervious to liquids and equally suited to the storage of powders and other pharmaceutical compounds. Stoneware jars found on the *Pandora* carry traces of medicinal products. Among the glass fragments from the *Sirius* was a flat oblong head stopper typical of those used for medicine bottles, and many thin glass pieces, possibly from phials

The **master** of a man-of-war was responsible for navigating and conducting the ship from port to port under the direction of the captain. He was required to accurately observe the appearance of coasts, rocks and shoals, with their depths of water and bearings, noting them in his journal. An extremely worn remnant of a depth sounding lead, found in Area 1, would have been part of the equipment in his care.

Among other duties, the **boatswain** was the officer in charge of the ship's boats, sails, rigging, colours, anchors, cables and cordage. So far three anchors are known to have been raised from the *Sirius* wreck site, only one these being lifted by the *Sirius* Project. The first was

*The pantograph, on a chart in Sydney Bay. Photograph by
Pat Baker, 1987.*
AUSTRALIAN BICENTENNIAL AUTHORITY

raised in 1905 and is now located in Macquarie Place, Sydney. The second, raised in 1973, is currently on display at Kingston, Norfolk Island along with a new wooden stock, jointly fabricated by Geoff Kimpton of the *Sirius* Project and Franklin Randall of the Norfolk Island Restoration Team during the *Sirius* Project in 1987.[49] The third anchor was raised on 4 March 1985 by the *Sirius* Project and is currently being conserved at the Norfolk Island Administrative Works Depot by a team of island personnel under the supervision of the Department of Materials Conservation at the Western Australian Maritime Museum.

All three anchors are old plan long-shanked anchors typical of the period. These anchors, generally with a wooden stock, had a long narrow shank, straight arms and very large palms which presented a good holding surface. Table 1, compiled by the authors, gives some idea of the comparative sizes of the *Sirius*' anchors.

TABLE 1

Date raised	Length of shank	Length of flukes	Span of palms	Thickness	Weight
1905	4.60 m [15'1"]		c. 1.52 m [c. 5']	Broken	
1973	4.62 m [15'1"]	1.75 m [5']	2.62 m [8'6"]	6.5 m [2⁹/₁₆"]	
1985	4.55 m [14'11"]	1.96 m [6'5"]	2.7 m [8'11"]		Est. 1.4±0.2 tonne [28 cwt]

As a further comparison, the standard specifications given by William Falconer in *A New Universal Dictionary of the Marine*, of 1815, for anchors made in His Majesty's Dockyards, are presented in Table 2, though no date is given.[50]

The number of anchors assigned to a vessel normally related to its class. Hence, according to 1809 tables in Falconer, a naval vessel such as the *Sirius*, rated for twenty guns, would be expected to carry '4 Bower anchors of 25 cwt [1.27 tonnes] each, 1 Stream anchor of 7½ cwt [381 kilograms] [and] 1 Kedge anchor of 3½ cwt [177 kilograms]'.[51] However, when she dragged her anchors in a storm off

Deal in 1787, heavier anchors were requested. It will be noted from Table 2, that anchors of 15 feet 1 inch (4.62 metres) weighed 34 hundredweight (1.73 tonnes). Thus, the two *Sirius* anchors of this length would correspond with this heavier weight. The estimated weight of 28 hundredweight (1.4 tonnes) for the third anchor is again in keeping with the fact that more substantial anchors were put on board.

Two small anchors still remain on the wreck site, in Areas 9 and 10 and a broken fluke, possibly from the anchor raised in 1905, lies in the gully at Area 1. The two anchors on the site are both broken, tending to suggest that they may have been on board as ballast. If there were four bower anchors on board the *Sirius* as per the normal complement for naval ships, then the fate of one still needs to be determined.

The **carpenter** was the officer appointed to examine and keep in

TABLE 2

Wt.	Length of shank	Length of flukes	Thickness of palms
28 cwt	14'4"	4'9¼"	1⅝"
31 cwt	14'9"	4'11"	1⅞"
33 cwt	15'	5'	1⅞"
34 cwt	15'1"	5'¼"	2"
35 cwt	15'2"	5'⅜"	2"

order the frame of the ship, together with its masts, yards, boats, all other wooden machinery, and stores committed to him by indenture from the surveyor of the dockyard. Especially, it was his duty to ensure that the ship was kept watertight, and to caulk the decks and planks whenever necessary. Hence, the carpenter would have been responsible for maintaining the pumps and stores such as the copper clinch rings, spare planking and sheathing nails.

The **gunner** was the officer in charge of all the ship's ordnance, together with the ordnance stores and ammunition.

So called from the first examples manufactured in 1778 by the Carron Iron Company in Scotland, the carronade was short and light in relation to the calibre. It usually had no trunnions. The 18-pounder was one of the original carronades introduced in 1779 to the forecastles and quarterdecks of British navy ships of from 28 to 44 guns. The 18-pounders had a maximum range of 1000 yards (914 metres) at 5 degrees elevation with a 1-pound 8-ounce (0.68 kilograms) charge. An 18-pounder long gun had a recoil of ten to twelve feet (3.05 to 3.66 metres). The carronade had a shorter recoil, but on truck carriages had a tendency to flip, so slide carriages were developed.

In 1781 all navy ships of two decks were to be supplied with 18-pounder carronades for their roundhouses. The *Berwick* was originally deemed suitable to carry four 18-pounder carronades. These early guns were 2 feet 4 inches (0.71 metres) long, measured from the beginning of the cascabel to the extremity of the muzzle, and weighed 8 hundredweight (406.4 kilograms), but the Navy Office was worried that this was too short:

> …carronades in general should be lengthened from 1 to 2 calibres, and as this alteration will not only carry them beyond the side, but remove the apprehension of endangering the hammacoes by fire and cannot add much to their present weight, we submit to their lordships whether the Board of Ordnance should not immediately direct the Carron Company to conform to such dimensions.[52]

By 1793, 3-foot 4-inch (1.02 metre) guns had replaced the old short ones.

In 1786 the *Sirius* was ordered to be supplied with six 18-pounder carronades, and at least one of these, retrieved from the wreck in 1985, was of the old length, 2 feet 4 inches (0.71 metres) with a cascabel of 12 inches (0.30 metres). There is no evidence to suggest that the *Sirius* retained the 18-pounder carronades from the *Berwick*. These would have been offloaded prior to her 1786 Deptford refit, and the *Sirius* was rearmed downstream at Longreach. But the 18-pounders received there were not necessarily new. It may be assumed that the 18-pounders would all have been carried on the upper deck, perhaps four on the quarterdeck and two on the forecastle.

The 18-pounder carronade raised from the *Sirius* wreck in 1985 bears on the left-hand trunnion the serial number 37,933, consistent with the Carron Company's numbers for that period, and an '18P' mark indicating an 18-pounder. A broad arrow is deeply incised on the cascabel, indicating that the gun had passed inspection and proof by the Ordnance Board. The numbers – 2–9, indicating 2 quarters and 9 pounds, part of the weight mark of the gun, are stamped into the reinforce just in front of the base ring. The preceding hundredweight number, which would have been an 8, is missing because of surface damage.

The gun exhibits extensive evidence of wear and damage incurred prior to the seabed development of a layer of concretion. The right-hand trunnion is badly worn, and there is damage to the cascabel, the muzzle, and the upper surface of the reinforce where a coat of arms might otherwise have appeared.[53] This damage may have occurred when material was thrown overboard at the time the *Sirius* was wrecked, because the 28-hundredweight (1.4-tonne) anchor was found lying directly on top of the gun on the seabed. Then again, the gun may not have been one of the ship's rating guns at all, but an old rejected gun, an item of ballast. A third possible explanation is that the gun was roughly handled while on the *Sirius*. Or it may be that the gun was in use despite having been worn and damaged prior to arriving on board the *Sirius*.

It seems unlikely that the gun had merely been used as ballast – contemporary evidence shows that two carronades were thrown overboard at the time of the wreck, and only one has so far been found. The gun was prone to damage during the voyages from 1787 to 1790. During the First Fleet voyage eight of the long guns from the main gun deck were taken down into the hold, and the damage may have occurred then. However, there is no indication that the 18-pounder carronades from the upper deck were struck down. Offloading the guns at Sydney could have caused some damage. There was, too, the voyage to and from Cape Town in October 1788 to May 1789, when the guns remaining on board might well have been thrown down into the hold. Nevertheless, the wear on the inside of the muzzle is more likely to have resulted from repeated use, so there remains the strong possibility that the *Sirius* was provided with heavily used guns in 1786.

The end of the American war saw the Board of Ordnance, as well as the Royal Navy, in need of a rest. There were not enough guns for all the ships, and many carried inadequately repaired old guns. In 1790, when a perceived Spanish threat prompted a Board of Ordnance survey of the fleet, twelve 74-gun ships were without guns or carriages.[54] It was generally considered dangerous to mix old and new guns in the same ship, as they would have differing powers of resistance, so if the 18-pounder was an old gun, it is likely that all the *Sirius*' guns were likewise.[55] Rust and wear were big problems. In one inspection in the 1780s two 18-pounders were reported as being large enough to take a 24-pound shot, and another was 'very wide at the muzzle'. Further study of the carronade's surface may be required to clarify the nature of the wear.

Two iron 6-pounders are mounted on truck carriages in front of the Norfolk Island Administration building in the New Military Barracks The 1926 Norfolk Island Administrator's Report states that the two guns are from the *Sirius*, and opinion has generally supported this view.

The overall length of each of the two guns is 1.97 metres (6 feet 6 inches), and they have the Blomefield pattern characteristics of a breech loop on the cascabel. The touch-hole patches are drilled for flintlock igniters. Both guns bear the incised broad arrow proof marks on the first reinforce and are marked on the second reinforce with the monogram of George III in relief. The trunnion diameter of 90 millimetres (3.54 inches) is consistent with the guns being 6-pounders: by 1716 the trunnions were equal in length and diameter to the bore, and in the eighteenth century the neck of the cascabel was equal to the bore in diameter.[56] The foresight patch of one gun is incised 1, and the other gun is incised 2.

The two guns were cleaned in 1985 as part of the *Sirius* Project, and at that time regular indentations were observed on the left-hand trunnion of the gun marked 1. Close observation and photography indicated that these were casting marks, normally expected on trunnions but previously unnoticed in this instance. The remains of three marks were visible, the upper indicating a serial number ending with the figures 27; the middle indicating the founders' name CARRON; and the lower the date 18-3.

It is quite clear from their appearance that neither gun had anything to do with the *Sirius*. To begin with, no Carron Company long guns were allowed on British navy ships between 1773 and 1795. In 1771 the Board of Ordnance noticed that a large proportion of Carron guns were bursting when tested, and began enquiries. This eventually resulted in a detailed investigation of Carron guns early in

1773, including special tests, and an assay of metal. As a result, large numbers were rejected, and the company was ordered not to proceed with casting any more. Carron guns already fitted to ships were removed. This prohibition on the casting of long guns was not removed until 1795.[57]

Secondly, the gun is obviously of the Blomefield pattern, having the ring to the top of the cascabel and the simple, curved, stronger breech, and lacking the heavy decorations of earlier guns. Major General Sir Thomas Blomefield was appointed Inspector of Artillery and Inspector of the Royal Brass Foundry at Woolwich in 1780. After 1786, Blomefield pattern guns of various calibres were made and tested at the Royal Arsenal. It is not clear exactly when the gun passed out of the experimental stage, but from about 1790 the draughts sent to the gunfounders were for guns of the new pattern.[58] By this time the *Sirius* was already on the rocks.

Thirdly, the figures 18-3 on the left-hand trunnion of one gun are very likely a date mark, referring to the date of casting of the piece. Compare the left-hand trunnion marks of the piece with the left hand trunnion marks on the following Carron guns located in Sydney:[59]

Gun	Location	Trunnion mark	Reinforce monogram
6-pounder	Norfolk Island	—·27 CARRON 18-3	GR3 – George III
24-pounder	Hyde Park	69990 CARRON 1806	GR – George Rex
32-pounder	Parramatta Park	70200 CARRON 1806	GR3 – George III
32-pounder	Parramatta Park	75625 CARRON 1810	GR3 – George III

Accepting that the two Norfolk Island cannon are not from the *Sirius*, it is pertinent to ask what their real origin is. Original documents refer to more than one 'great' gun's presence on the island during the first settlement. However, when the island was abandoned in 1814 there was concern that the French might make use of any remaining facilities to establish themselves there, so everything that was considered likely to be of use to them was removed. Cannon would surely be the first such objects removed.

The second British convict settlement on Norfolk Island began in 1825, and lasted until 1855. As might be expected of such a settlement, it was equipped with several cannon. An 1838 illustration of the settlement shows two long guns mounted in front of Government House. A contemporary document states that Captain Alexander Maconochie, the reforming superintendent, moved them to the New Military Barracks in 1841.[60] A photograph dated around 1895 shows, lying on the ground in front of the New Military Barracks, two cannon, which look like the ones now mounted. At the abandonment of the second settlement there was not the same need to clear the island of old cannon. The British government well knew of the impending arrival of the friendly Pitcairners. Thus the probability is that the guns arrived on the island in or soon after 1825, and have remained there since.

A final question is that of the fate of the *Sirius*' complement of guns. The *Sirius* left Britain in 1787 with her own guns and some intended for the garrison at Sydney. The garrison guns, and some of her own guns, were offloaded on arrival at Sydney, and it is not clear how many guns were on board when the vessel left for Norfolk Island.

The record indicates what happened to some of them. Two carronades are recorded as having fallen overboard when the *Sirius* struck the reef. All the other guns were reportedly salvaged in 1791. Four of these were used to arm the *Marquis Cornwallis* in 1796. Five of the swivel guns were provided as ballast to the colonial schooner *Francis* in 1794. There is also reference to eight 6-pounders being returned to Sydney.[61]

A variety of ammunition was found on the *Sirius* wreck site, concentrated in several distinct areas. In the Area 1 gully, concentrations of small iron shot were heavily concreted together, while in Areas 8 and 12 larger round shot or cannon balls were located.

Grape shot and remains of canvas bag in concretion. Photograph by Pat Baker, 1987.
AUSTRALIAN BICENTENNIAL AUTHORITY

Evidence of canvas and marling around some of the small iron shot indicated this to be grape shot, so named because of its resemblance to a bunch of grapes. Grape shot consists of a number of small iron balls arranged around a central iron column in a thick canvas bag. The column is attached to a base at the bottom of the bag and the neck of the bag securely tied with strong cord. To keep the shot from moving, tarred marline made of two to four strands of cord is drawn around the balls, giving the bag a quilted appearance. A rope grommet is then formed at the top by which it can be carried or hung on small hooks next to the guns. Finally, the shot is painted with two coats of black paint to preserve it, except for the disc and stem, generally treated with red ochre.

For sea service, quilted grape shot was filled with nine balls only, irrespective of the calibre of the gun.[62] The weight of each shot, however, varied with respect to the size or poundage of the gun from which it was to be fired. Thus, for an 18-pounder, each shot would weigh 1 pound 8 ounces (681 grams), giving a total weight of 19 pounds 15½ ounces (9.06 kilograms) for the grape shot. Likewise, for a 6-pounder gun, each ball would weigh 8 ounces (227 grams), giving a total weight of 5 pounds 8½ ounces (2.51 kilograms).[63]

The small shot from the *Sirius* falls into three groups with mean diameters of 24 millimetres, 34 millimetres and 39 millimetres. From tables in Wilkinson-Latham's *British Artillery on Land and Sea 1790-1820*,[64] giving the weights of shot and their relationship to particular types of ammunition and ordnance, it is possible to make some assessment of the type of ammunition carried on the *Sirius*. The original mass of a cast iron ball of 39 millimetres diameter would be 226.7 grams, based on a density for cast iron of 7.3. This effectively corresponds to the weight given for grape shot balls used with a 6-pounder gun, which suggests these balls were used for that purpose, rather than as ammunition for the carronades.

The 34-millimetre balls, however, would originally have weighed 150 grams (about 5¼ ounces) making them close to the 6-ounce balls used in English case shot for 18-pounder carronades. The 24-millimetre balls, at an original weight of 52.8 grams (about 2 ounces), would likewise correspond to the size of case or canister shot for 6-pounder guns. Case shot consisted of a cylindrical tin canister, made to fit the calibre of the particular ordnance, which was filled with shot and sealed at the base with a wooden plug. The plug was then forced into a cartridge bag and tied. The whole was then enclosed in another bag and tied with gut.[65] The case shot for the 6-pounder guns contained 40 balls in each case and those for the 18-pounder carronades 31 balls per case.

Only a small number of cannon balls were recovered from the wreck site, but two groups can be isolated, based on the size of the balls. One group had diameters ranging from 85 millimetres to 94 millimetres, and the other 127 millimetres to 131 millimetres. Given that the standard calibre of a 6-pounder gun is 93 millimetres (3.668 inches),[66] the first group of shot are likely to have been used with guns of this size. The slightly larger 94-millimetre shot would not have been a problem, since it was anticipated that iron shot would suffer some degree of corrosion or rusting on board ship, which would marginally reduce the size of the balls over time.

The larger shot would have had weights of 17⅕ pounds (7.8 kilograms) for the 127-millimetre shot; 17½ pounds (8 kilograms) for the 128-millimetre shot; and 18½ pounds (8.4 kilograms) for the

Small lead shot. Photograph by Pat Baker, 1987
AUSTRALIAN BICENTENNIAL AUTHORITY

131-millimetre shot. These weights, therefore, correspond with the size of shot required for the 18-pounder carronades with calibres of 5.16 inches (131 millimetres).

The **armourer** is the officer appointed by warrant to clean and keep in repair the muskets, pistols and cutlasses, and to do all the kinds of smith-work of a ship of war. In Area 8 of the wreck site, artefacts were located which gave a clue to the type of small arms carried on board the *Sirius*. A brass wrist escutcheon and three trumpet-shaped ramrod pipes were all clearly associated with Short Land Pattern muskets,[67] as are two brass trigger guards in the Norfolk Island Museum collection. The First Fleet took along 200 short land muskets and twelve sergeants' carbines, probably Grenadier Sergeants' Carbines with bayonets,[68] for the marines.

The Short Land Pattern musket was officially sanctioned as an infantry musket by royal warrant in June 1768, although it had been in use before that date.[69] Its overall length was 58⅛ inches (1.5 metres), its barrel length 42 inches (1.06 metres), and its calibre about 0.78 inches (19.8 millimetres). The wrist escutcheon was a typical feature of Land Pattern muskets in the eighteenth century and the trumpet-shaped upper ramrod pipes were a fixture designed to accommodate steel rather than wooden, brass-tipped ramrods.

Brass furniture for firearms was manufactured by brass founders in London or Birmingham according to patterns issued by the Board of Ordnance. The finished components would be sent either to the board's contractors or directly to the central depot, the Tower of London. From there, sets of components were distributed to a relatively small number of London gun makers known as 'rough stockers and setters up' who smoothed and finished the rough wooden stock blanks and assembled the weapons.[70] The completed firearms were then delivered to the Tower of London and issued against specific requisitions.

At the time the *Sirius* set sail from England two types of Land Pattern musket were in issue: Long and Short Land muskets, the main structural difference being one of barrel length – 46 inches (1.17 metres) compared to 42 inches (1.06 metres). Short Land muskets were, however, being used in most regiments by this time, replacing the Long Land muskets. The latter were frequently shortened owing to wear, damage or a desire to update them.

Two gunflints were also found in Area 8 along with a heavy concentration of musket balls and lead shot. The small arms ammunition failed to come aboard the *Sirius* in London[71] and Phillip had to purchase 10 000 musket balls in Rio de Janeiro.[72] Of a total of 707 shot, 61 per cent had a diameter between 17 millimetres (0.66 inches) and 19 millimetres (0.75 inches). The larger balls were thus compatible with the 0.78 inches (19.8-millimetre) calibre of the Short Land Pattern muskets while the smaller ones would have been suitable for the Sergeants' Carbines which had a calibre of about 0.65 inches (16.5 millimetres).[73] Interestingly, 33 per cent of the shot had a diameter between 12 millimetres (0.47 inches) and 14 millimetres (0.55 inches) tending to suggest an even smaller calibre firearm.[74] Some of the balls in this group had a small protrusion or lip which seems to indicate that they would have been used as cartridge shot.[75] A cartridge of twisted paper containing powder would have been tied to the lip of the musket ball, the end being bitten off with the teeth before priming and loading.[76] Such ammunition, with small bird shot added to the cartridge, was commonly used with fowling pieces or shotguns for shooting birds or game. Indeed, a small quantity of bird or pistol shot was recovered from concretions in Area 2–3.

Only a few items have so far been recovered which relate to the **personal belongings or uniforms** of the people on board the *Sirius*. Many of these came from Areas 7, 8 and 12. Two brass shoulder-belt plates from Areas 7 and 8, decorated with an anchor, would appear to be from the uniforms of officers of the Royal Marines. They would have been attached to the 2-inch-wide white leather belt worn after 1775 over the right shoulder to hold a sword on the left-hand side.[77] In 1784, buckles with slides were officially ordered but were soon withdrawn in favour of 'oval plates', made of gilt or brass generally with an anchor design.[78]

Five pewter buttons, one with an anchor motif, and a decorated flat brass button, all from Area 8, might also be associated with the Marines. While officers generally had gilt buttons on their uniforms, other ranks had simple pewter buttons, decorated with an incised fouled anchor. A small oval brass buckle from Area 12 could well have belonged to a shoe, part of a leather shoe sole being found in the same vicinity.

Probably the most interesting discovery, however, was in Area 1. Among a collection of flint pebble ballast and heavily concreted iron shot, a stone hatchet head was found. It was distinguished from accompanying flint ballast pebbles by its unnaturally shaped edge. Accurate identification of the tool was crucial to the determination of its origin and the explanation of how it came to be among the remains of the *Sirius*.

It was conceivable that the Thames flint ballast that the ship was carrying could contain a stone axe. Alternatively, a member of the crew may have acquired it as a curiosity when the vessel was stationed in Sydney, or from Cape Town during a voyage to procure grain. Stone axes have been found on Norfolk Island, in Emily Bay, 450 metres from the wreck site, which predate Cook's visit and indicate a visit by Pacific voyagers around AD 900–1100.[79] Thus the axe could possibly have related to earlier pre-European visits to the island.

Examination of the artefact by Australian prehistorians, however, indicates that it is a tool made and used by Australian Aborigines, probably originating from a source somewhere in New South Wales.[80] The tool has been fashioned from a flattish pebble, probably obtained from a creek or river bed. One end of the pebble has been ground on two sides to form a sharp cutting edge suitable for woodworking. Stone hatchets were commonly used to remove bark from trees and for chopping or splitting wood.

A wrap-around handle, made of wood that could be easily bent without undue fracture of the wood fibres, would have been attached to the hatchet head.[81] Bradley, Hunter and Surgeon White all commented on the Aboriginal use of various gums, or 'adhesives', to bond stone and wood in the manufacture of spears and tools.[82] An analysis of the surface residue on the *Sirius* hatchet head was thus undertaken in order to determine the type of natural bonding substance used to secure the hatchet handle, formerly thought to be beeswax.[83] This analysis shows the compound to be a mixture of saturated and unsaturated fatty acids.[84] This suggests that a plant resin has been combined with an animal product filler, such as kangaroo dung, but the precise origin of the compounds has yet to be determined.

The British government had sent out with the First Fleet a miscellany of curios to entice favourable response from the Aborigines, including nine casks of ironmongery, ten cases of beads, and eleven looking-glasses.[85] Captain Hunter frequently made gifts of iron hatchets during his explorations in New South Wales. William Bradley described the stone hatchets used by the Aborigines to make canoes and shields from trees in his journal in October 1788:

> The Stone Hatchet is made of a hard stone much like Flint, sharpened at the edge, secured to a stick about 2 feet long by fixing in with Gum & lashings & is a miserable blunt tool.[86]

Hunter appears not to have noticed Aboriginal hatchets in the early months, although he did refer to notches cut in the bark of trees. Aboriginal implements were of great interest to the crews of British vessels, and their theft by Europeans led to problems, as Phillip observed during a survey in November 1788:

> ...The Natives now around us more than they did when we first landed, and which I impute to the Robberies committed on them

by the Convicts, who steal their spears and Fiz-gigs, which they frequently leave in their huts when they go out a fishing, and which the people belonging to the Transports purchase, though every possible precaution has been taken to prevent it: this the Natives revenge by attacking any Stragglers they meet, and one Convict has been killed since the *Sirius* sailed.[87]

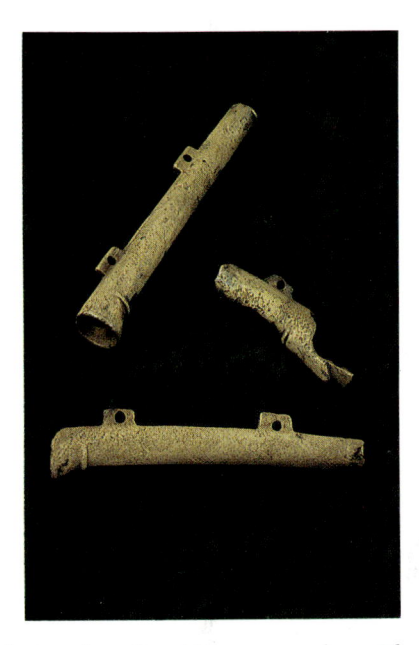

Ramrod pipes from Land Pattern muskets. Photograph by Pat Baker, 1987
AUSTRALIAN BICENTENNIAL AUTHORITY

CHAPTER 10
Conclusion

Although the *Sirius* Project is not yet complete, almost all of its original aims have now been achieved. The site has been declared and thus given the full protection of the commonwealth Historic Shipwrecks Act. Divers are free to swim on the *Sirius* wreck, but cannot legally remove material without a permit from the Department of Arts, Sport, Environment, Tourism and Territories. The site has been surveyed and described. Exposed and loose material has been removed from the site by maritime archaeologists, recorded and analysed. The objects raised have been or are in the process of being conserved by Norfolk Islanders and scientists from the Western Australian Maritime Museum. The material is housed in the care of Robert Varman, the curator on Norfolk Island, with the exception of items temporarily in Australia for exhibition or conservation. A register has been developed of material raised from the wreck prior to the *Sirius* Project's investigations. The Norfolk Island government is acting upon advice from the Museums Association of Australia and the Western Australian Maritime Museum on the longer term conservation, housing, and display of the collection.

The communities of Norfolk Island and mainland Australia have been made more aware of the historical and archaeological significance of the *Sirius*' remains in the short term by means of public lectures and media releases. Some forty members of the press attended the press conference arranged in Sydney immediately after the 1987 expedition to the *Sirius* site was completed, an indication of the strong public interest in the project. Longer term arrangements have included assistance in the production of a documentary film by Richard Swansborough, and academic progress reports, as well as this book, which describes the project's progress to date. The inclusion of *Sirius* Project material in two national travelling exhibitions – the Australian Bicentennial Exhibition and the 'Shipwreck!' exhibition – is also contributing to that community awareness.

The *Sirius* Project, as first conceived, was scheduled for completion in 1987, and the Australian Bicentennial Authority's funding followed this schedule.

But several challenges remain. The historical and archaeological questions posed in 1987, the principal archaeological deposit was found, invite further exploration; what was the *Sirius'* condition and suitability at the commencement of the First Fleet voyage, and what was involved in the process of transformation from warship to archaeological site? To pursue these questions the *Sirius* Project is planning a final expedition to Norfolk Island in October 1988. Archaeologists will concentrate on gathering more information from objects about the condition and suitability of the *Sirius*. A trench will be cut through the ballast mound to establish the nature and level of preservation of the underlying material.

Of great importance to the people of Norfolk Island is the development of a museum on Norfolk Island, which can be used as an interpretive centre for the *Sirius* collection. There are no funds for this purpose in the *Sirius* Project, but the Norfolk Island government has selected a building and is putting its plans into effect.

Who is to own and control the objects raised by the *Sirius* Project? The expedition in 1987 revealed a rich variety of artefacts on the *Sirius* wreck site. The *Sirius* Project passed this material into the care of the Norfolk Island government. However, an element of uncertainty arose as to control – whether the collected objects would remain on Norfolk Island or be taken to a central location on the Australian mainland. Prior to the *Sirius* Project no commonwealth departments had indicated any desire to collect relics from historic shipwrecks, except in the case of the Dutch wrecks off Western Australia, and then only a small collection of duplicated material, to which the Western Australian government had formally agreed under a special arrangement, was considered. At the beginning of the *Sirius* Project the Department of Arts, Heritage and Environment assured project members that it had no intention of removing *Sirius* material from Norfolk Island, and its representative, Jennifer Amess, passed excavated objects into the care of the Norfolk Island government. When the Australian Bicentennial Authority sought the approval of the Norfolk Island government to temporarily remove material for the two bicentennial-year travelling exhibitions, the request was backed up by an assurance by the then Minister of the Department of Arts, Heritage and Environment, Barry Cohen, that all objects would be returned to Norfolk Island.

Seeking funds for an additional, final expedition to the *Sirius* wreck site, the *Sirius* Project had discussions with potential sponsors. The museum then raised the issues of ownership and custody. The British government claims ownership of Admiralty wrecks irrespective of the location and period since wreckage, but the Australian government accepts these claims and seeks transfer of ownership. Under Australia's Historic Shipwrecks Act the Minister has the power to act to preserve objects, to exhibit them, to place them in a collection, and to make them available for study. The Norfolk Island government and community grew concerned that the objects in the travelling exhibitions would not be returned, and that the objects raised by a future *Sirius* Project expedition would be taken from the island. In such an atmosphere another expedition to complete the project could not be contemplated.

Gary Punch, the new minister, resolved the situation when he announced that the *Sirius* objects would be returned to Norfolk Island at the conclusion of the travelling exhibitions. This opened the way for the *Sirius* Project's planned expedition to complete activities in October 1988. This timing should coincide with the visit to Australia of the present HMS *Sirius*. The expedition is funded by British Airways and administered by the Norfolk Island government in consultation with the Department of Arts, Sport, Environment, Tourism and Territories, as an Australian Bicentennial Authority endorsed project. The *Sirius* Project, a successful initiative of the Department of Arts, Heritage and Environment, and the Australian Bicentennial Authority, is now entering a new phase of increased involvement by the Norfolk Island community.

The higher level of recognition of and support for Norfolk Island's maritime heritage is timely. The islanders' expressions of concern had signified great public awareness of and interest in historical relics, an acceptance of maritime archaeological material as legitimate historical evidence and a recognition of the value of linking the disciplines of archaeology and history to obtain a fuller picture of the past. This book in itself is a demonstration of the complementary nature of archaeology and history, showing how in one instance the standard historical record of significant events in Australian history has been enlivened by the retrieval and analysis of archaeological material, and how that record has in turn shed light on the function of each artefact retrieved.

Glossary

Air scuttles: small hatchways cut for ventilation through a ship's deck.
Backstay stools: planking projecting from the sides of sailing vessels, to which the ends of backstays are made fast.
Batten bulkhead: partition built up between two decks using straight hoops of casks or other light planking.
Braces: lugs projecting from the after side of the stern to support the rudder. Each brace is bored out to receive the corresponding pintle.
Bream: to burn off accretions from a ship's bottom.
Butt bolts: fastening running through planking close to joining ends of planks.
Cants: pieces of wood laid on the deck to support erections.
Cascabel: the knob at the rear end of a cannon.
Chain cable: anchor cable consisting of iron links.
Cheeks: side pieces by which the cutwater is secured to the bows of the ship.
Clinch bolt: a long through fastening used by wooden shipbuilders having its end rivetted over a washer or clinch ring. It is used for fastening scarphed joints, stems, deadwoods, keelsons and knees.
Coak: the metal hole or bearing in a sheave through which the pin runs.
Cro-jack yard: cross-jack yard – the yard on the mizzenmast supporting the cross-jack sail. The lowest of the yards on the mizzenmast.
Crosspieces: rails of timber connecting two knightheads or two bitts.
Cutter: a ship's boat, broader, deeper and shorter than a pinnace. They are fitter for sailing, and commonly employed in carrying light stores, provisions and passengers to and from the ships.
Deadeyes: stout disks of hard wood, strapped with rope, through which holes are pierced for the reception of lanyards. They are used as blocks to connect shrouds and chainplates.
Deadwood: solid timbers bolted on top of the keel in the stem and stern of a vessel.
Easy rounded bilge: refers to the turn of bilge – the lower outer part of the bilge where the curvature is greatest. The turn from the flat of the bottom to the upward rise of the sides.
Fetch: the distance from the weather shore where the formation of waves commences.
Fiddle head: a substitute for the traditional figurehead in the form of a scroll. It is generally called fiddle head when the scroll turns outward, and billet head when it turns inward.
Figure: see Head.
Fish: a long piece of oak, concave on one side, used to strengthen masts after damage or when it became necessary to carry an extra press of sail.
Fish tackle fall: the hauling part of the rope used in a tackle to hoist the flukes of the anchor.
Full entrance: the entrance is the immersed part of the hull forward of the cross section of greatest area. A vessel has a full entrance when the extremities of the waterlines at load line level are strongly convex and the ends of the curve of sectional areas are full, indicating that displacement is carried well forward.
Galleries: balconies over the stern of ships with access from the stern windows.
Gallantmast: topgallant mast – the mast next above a topmast, and which may consist of a separate spar or a single stick with the topmast.
Grown or compass timbers: naturally crooked pieces of wood used for the framing of vessels.
Gudgeon: see Brace.
Halfport: one of two shutters, upper and lower, which close a porthole.

GLOSSARY

Hanging or lodging knee: wooden knee having one leg fastened against the upright side or the under side of a beam and the other leg against the ship's side.

Hawsepieces: the foremost timbers of the ship.

Head: an ornamental figure erected on the continuation of a ship's stem. The whole forepart of a ship including the bows.

Headledges: the athwartship coamings at the forward and after ends of a hatchway.

Lag bolts: screws used to fasten the pintles and braces to the rudder and sternpost.

Light room: a room contiguous to the magazine filling room, with the purpose of providing light when required.

Limber boards: short pieces of board forming the upper part of the limber passage – the limber passage allows water to flow to the well – and made portable so that any obstruction in the passage can be cleared away.

Magazine filling room: a close room built in the fore or after part of a ship's hold, to contain the gunpowder used in battle. It is strongly secured against fire, and no person is allowed to enter it with a light or candle.

Manger boards: a low partition extending athwartships immediately abaft the hawseholes. It serves to hinder the passage aft of water which may come in at the hawseholes or from the cable when heaving in. The water thus prevented from running aft is returned to the sea by the manger scuppers.

Mast hoops: iron bands used for binding together the several pieces of a made mast.

Nesting of boats: the stowage of boats one inside the other after removing the thwarts, making for great economy of space.

Pintles: heavy pins on the forward edge of the rudder frame, by which the rudder is hinged to the sternpost around which it pivots.

Planipieces: planeshear, plankshear – continuous planking covering the timber heads and forming a shelf below the gunwale.

Port tack: the direction of a vessel's head with regard to the trim of its sails; on the port tack, it has the wind on the port side.

Pulley block sheaves: grooved wheels over which ropes pass. The sheave, which is bushed, rotates upon the pin.

Quarter galleries: ornamented projections from the quarters of a square-sterned ship, intended to decorate and provide a finish to the quarters.

Rabbet of keel: a recess on the edge of the keel to protect the plank ends and permit caulking.

Raft ports: square holes cut immediately under the counter to receive long pieces of timber such as masts for transportation.

Rails: curved pieces of timber, extending from the bows on each side to the continuation of the ship's stem, to support the knee of the head and the ornamental figure.

Rake: the overhang of a vessel forward.

Ranges: large cleats with two arms bolted in the waist of a sailing ship to which tacks and bow lines are attached.

Riding bitts: heavy wooden posts for fastening anchor cables.

Rubboard: an external stiffener extending longitudinally on the sides of a vessel a short distance above the water line to protect it against damage from quay-walls and other vessels.

Scarph: to join the ends of two timbers so as to form a continuous piece in appearance.

Shackle: a U-shaped metal fitting with a pin across the throat, used as a connection between lengths of chain, or to attach other fittings.

Sheathing tacks: small sharp-ended fastenings for fixing copper sheets to hulls for protection against ship worms and marine growths.

Shifts: contrivances for moving heavy objects about in a ship.

Spritsail yard: a yard hanging under the bowsprit to support a sail.

Square tuck: tuck is the name given to that part of the ship where the ends of the bottom planks are collected together immediately under the stern or counter. A square tuck is terminated above by the wing transom, and below and on each side by the fashion pieces.

Standards: inverted knee timbers placed above instead of beneath the deck.

Stocks: a number of wooden blocks ranged parallel to each other at convenient distances, and gradually declining towards the water.

Stopper bolts: ring-bolts in the deck to which are fastened stoppers – short pieces of rope used to suspend weighty bodies such as anchors, or to retain a cable in a fixed position.

Top chains: chains to sling the lower yards in time of battle.

Topmast: the spar next above a lower mast and below the topgallant mast in a square rigger.

Top riders: interior ribs fixed opposite to the upper parts of some of the ship's existing ribs to strengthen the frame.

Tumblehome: that part of a ship's side that falls inward above the extreme breadth.

Wale scuttles: small square ports cut in the lids of gun-deck ports for ventilation when the lids had to be closed in rough weather.

Weather bow: the forward quarter of a ship which is on the windward side.

Windlass: a large cylindrical piece of wood, supported by frames at each end, and turned by levers to hoist anchors.

Wing transom: a transverse timber which extends between the fashion pieces, crossing in front of the sternpost near the head. In square-sterned ships it forms the base of the stern.

References

Chapter 1

[1] Bateson, Charles, *The Convict Ships*, (Brown Son & Ferguson, Glasgow, 1959)) p. 3.
[2] Frost, Alan, *Arthur Phillip 1738–1814: His Voyaging* (Oxford University Press, Melbourne, 1987) pp. 95, 97.
[3] Frost, *op. cit.*, p. 125.
[4] The war was said to have cost Britain £100 million. See Rudé, George, *Revolutionary Europe 1783–1815* (Collins, London, 1964) p. 59.
[5] The reasons for this are discussed in Ashton, T.S., *Economic Fluctuations* (Oxford University Press, Oxford, 1959) pp. 160–161.
[6] 'Criteria Suggested for Establishing a Penal Settlement, August 1785 (Report of the Transportation [Beauchamp] Select Committee)', *House of Commons Journal*, vol. 40, 1785, pp. 1161–4: quoted in Evans, Lloyd and Nicholls, Paul, *Convicts and Colonial Society 1788–1868*, second edition (Macmillan, Melbourne, 1984) pp. 15–18.
[7] Porter, Roy, *English Society in the Eighteenth Century* (Penguin, England, 1982) p. 19.
[8] Most other European countries had a larger percentage of their population as peasantry or serfs, subsisting or supporting themselves from the land. See Mathias, Peter, *The First Industrial Nation: An Economic History of Britain 1700–1914*, second edition (Methuen, London and New York, 1969. Second edition 1983) pp. 27–29.
[9] Quoted in Porter, *op. cit.*, pp. 67–68.
[10] Mathias, *op. cit.*, p. 29.
[11] See Gregory King's estimate of the population and wealth of England and Wales, calculated for 1688 in Mathias, *op. cit.*, p. 24.
[12] Porter, *op. cit.*, p. 35.
[13] *Ibid.*, p. 51.
[14] Mathias, *op. cit.*, p. 46.
[15] Kennedy, Paul M., *The Rise and Fall of British Naval Mastery* (Allen Lane, 1976. Macmillan, London, 1983 edition), p. 71.
[16] A higher premium was placed on the functional efficiency of the navy because the importance of the navy's role received more general recognition at Westminster. See Mathias, *op. cit.*, p. 46.
[17] *Ibid.*, p. 45.
[18] Ashton, *op. cit.*, p. 28.
[19] Mathias, *op. cit.*, pp. 48–49.
[20] Porter, *op. cit.*, p. 65.
[21] *Ibid.*, p. 66.
[22] Frost, *op. cit.*, pp. 7, 13, 44.
[23] Schaffer, Simon, 'Scientific Instruments and their Public', in Porter, Roy *et al.*, *Science and Profit in Eighteenth Century London* (Whipple Museum of the History of Science, Cambridge, 1985) p. 10.
[24] Josiah Wedgewood was one such benefactor. See Schaffer, *op. cit.*, p. 12.
[25] The Swiss writer B.L. de Muralt (1725) thought the *mot juste* for the English was 'fierce'. Quoted in Porter, *op. cit.*, p. 270.
[26] Porter, *op. cit.*, pp. 53–55; 271.
[27] *Ibid.*, p. 53.
[28] Ashton, *op. cit.*
[29] Porter, *op. cit.*, p. 53.
[30] Universal access to land no longer existed and, where employment opportunities in agriculture did not expand with increasing rural populations, the extra children in the villages had to seek non-agricultural work, in the villages, in the nearby towns or in the city, when they grew up. Mathias, *op. cit.*, pp. 56–59. See also Rudé, *op. cit.*, p. 25.

[31] To feed the expanding nation, 'mixed farming' was introduced and this required more labour. Mathias, 1969, p. 57.
[32] Many of the migrants were Britons unable to make a decent livelihood in their own land and foreign refugees who had sought asylum in England for religious and other reasons. See George, M. Dorothy, *London Life in the Eighteenth Century* (Penguin, London, 1925; Peregrine edition 1966) p. 131.
[33] The seed from a tropical American tree from which cocoa and chocolate are made.
[34] Extract from Beauchamp Select Committee Report. Cited in Evans and Nicholls, *op. cit.*, p. 16.
[35] George, *op. cit.*, pp. 148–150. See also Evans and Nicholls, *op. cit.*, p. 16.
[36] Fieldhouse, D. K., *The Colonial Empires: a Comparative Survey from the Eighteenth Century* (Germany, 1965; English edition, Weidenfeld and Nicholson, London, 1966) p. 59.
[37] Frost, Alan, *Convicts and Empire: a Naval Question 1776–1811* (Oxford University Press, Melbourne, 1980) p. 58.
[38] Murphy, B., *A History of the British Economy 1086–1970* (London, 1973) Quoted in Kennedy, *op. cit.*, p. 21.
[39] Kennedy, *op. cit.*, p. 23.
[40] Mathias, *op. cit.*, p. 79.
[41] Clarke, J.J., 'The Merchant Marine and the Navy: A Note on the Mahan Hypothesis', *Royal United Services Institution Journal*, CXII, 646 (May 1967), quoted in Kennedy, *op. cit.* p. 8.
[42] Mathias, *op. cit.*, p. 85.
[43] Davis, Ralph, *The Rise of the English Shipping Industry in the Seventeenth and Eighteenth Centuries* (Macmillan, 1962; National Maritime Museum Modern Maritime Classics Reprint No. 3, 1972) p. 286. See also Fayle, C. E., *A Short History of the World's Shipping Industry* (Allen & Unwin, London, 1933) p. 215.
[44] Fayle, *ibid.*
[45] Mathias, *op. cit.*, p. 86; Ashton, *op. cit.* p. 185.
[46] Mathias, *op. cit.*, p. 86.
[47] Ashton, *op. cit.* p. 71.
[48] Ashton, 1959, p. 71; Davis, 1962, p. 42.
[49] Abell, Westcott, Sir, *The Shipwright's Trade* (Conway Maritime Press, London, 1948. 1981 impression) p. 95.
[50] Phillips-Birt, Douglas, *The Building of Boats* (Maurice Michael, Partridge Green, England, 1979) p. 165.
[51] Albion, Robert, G., 'The Timber Problem of the Royal Navy, 1652–1862', *The Mariner's Mirror*, 38 (1952), pp. 4–22.
[52] Mitchell, R.J. and Leys, M.D.R., *A History of London Life* (Longmans, 1958; Pelican Books, 1963) p. 80.
[53] Davis, *op. cit.*, p. 213.
[54] Malone, Joseph, J., 'England and the Baltic Naval Stores Trade in the Seventeenth and Eighteenth Centuries', *The Mariner's Mirror*, 58, (1972), pp. 375–395 pp. 388–389.
[55] Davis, *op. cit.*, pp. 219–227.
[56] *Ibid*, p. 221.
[57] Dodds and Moore, *op. cit.*, p. 19.
[58] Davis, *op. cit.*, p. 221.
[59] *Ibid.*
[60] Albion, *op. cit.*, p. 7; Mathias, *op. cit.*, p. 77.
[61] Mathias, *op. cit.*, p. 79.
[62] Kennedy, *op. cit.*, p. 113.
[63] Fieldhouse, *op. cit.*, p. 76.
[64] Fayle, *op. cit.*, p. 193.
[65] Mathias, *op. cit.*, pp. 40-41.
[66] Porter, 1982, p. 218.
[67] Fayle, *op. cit.*, p. 195.
[68] Syrett, D., *Shipping and the American War 1775–1783* (London, 1970), quoted in Kennedy, *op. cit.*, p. 114.

[69] Frost, 1980, pp. 66 ff.
[70] Syrett, David, 'The Navy Board and Merchant Shipowners during the American War, 1776–1783', *The American Neptune*, XLVII, 1 (1987), pp. 5–13.
[71] Syrett, *op. cit.*, p. 7.
[72] *Ibid.*, p. 12.
[73] *Ibid.*
[74] Chalmers, George, (c. 1784), quoted in Ashton, *op. cit.*, p. 62.
[75] Kennedy, *op. cit.*, p. 117.
[76] Ashton, *op. cit.*, p. 62.
[77] Mathias, *op. cit.*, pp. 94–95.
[78] *Ibid.*, pp. 96–97.
[79] Rousseau, Jean-Jacques, *The Social Contract and Discourses* (Dent, London and Melbourne, G.D.H. Cole, J.H. Brumfitt and John C. Hall revised edition, 1973) pp. 44–113.
[80] Brady, Terence and Jones, Evan, *The Fight against Slavery* (British Broadcasting Corporation, London, 1975) p. 66.
[81] Brady and Jones, *op. cit.*, p. 53.
[82] Porter, *op. cit.*, p. 136.
[83] See Ashton, *op. cit.*, and George, *op. cit.*
[84] Mathias, *op. cit.*, p. 42; Ashton, *op. cit.*, p. 187 gives a total of 237 000 in the armed forces in 1782.
[85] Ashton, *op. cit.*, pp. 52–53.
[86] *Ibid.*, p.160.
[87] George, *op. cit.*, p. 28.
[88] Porter, *op. cit.*, p. 114.
[89] Hughes, Robert, *The Fatal Shore: a History of the Transportation of Convicts to Australia, 1787–1868* (Collins Harvill, London, 1987) p. 27.
[90] Extract from Beauchamp Select Committee Report, 1785, quoted in Evans and Nicholls, *op. cit.*, p. 15.
[91] Frost, 1980, p. 77.
[92] *Ibid.*, pp. 80 ff
[93] Rudé, *op. cit.*, p. 59.
[94] Frost, 1980, pp. 99–101.
[95] Kennedy, *op. cit.*, p. 121.
[96] Frost, 1980, *op. cit.*, p. 70.
[97] Philips, C.H., *The East India Company 1784–1834* (Manchester University Press, 1940. Reprinted with minor corrections, 1961) p. 14.
[98] *Ibid.* p. 67.
[99] Crowhurst, R.P., 'The Admiralty and the Convoy System in the Seven Years War', *The Mariner's Mirror*, 57, 2 (1971), pp. 163–173.
[100] Letter from Lord Sydney to the Lords Commissioner of the Treasury, dated 18 August 1786, reprinted in Martin, Ged, (ed.), *The Founding of Australia: the Argument About Australia's Origins.* (Hale & Iremonger, Sydney, 1978) p. 22.
[101] Phillip, Arthur, *et al.*, *The Voyage to Botany Bay.*. (Stockdale, London, 1789. Australiana Facsimile Editions, Hutchinson, Australia, 1982) p. 5.
[102] Blainey, Geoffrey, *The Tyranny of Distance: How Distance Shaped Australia's History.* (Sun Books, Melbourne, 1966) pp. IX, 16 ff.
[103] 'Heads of a Plan', reprinted in Martin, *op. cit.*, p. 28.
[104] Blainey, *op. cit.*, p. 28.
[105] *Ibid.*, p. 32.
[106] *Ibid.* p. 30. See also Frost, 1980, *op. cit.*, pp. 123–124.
[107] Bolton, G.C., 'Broken reeds and smoking flax.', in Martin, *op. cit.*, pp. 115–121; Shaw, A.G.L., 'The hollow conqueror and the tyranny of distance', in Martin, *op. cit.*, pp. 122–130.
[108] Bolton, G.C., 'The hollow conqueror: flax and the foundation of Australia', in Martin, *op. cit.*, p. 98.
[109] Matra and Young's proposals are reprinted in Martin, *op. cit.*, pp. 9–21. For more detailed discussion of these and other proposals, see Frost, 1980, pp. 18–32.

[110] Fry, H.T., '"Cathay and the way thither": the background to Botany Bay', in Martin, *op. cit.*, pp. 186–208.
[111] Martin, Ged., 'A London newspaper on the founding of Botany Bay, August 1786–May 1787', in Martin, *op. cit.*, pp. 169–184.
[112] Atkinson, A., 'Whigs and Tories and Botany Bay', in Martin, *op. cit.*, pp. 186–208.
[113] Frost, 1980 and Frost, Alan, 'Towards Australia: the Coming of the Europeans 1400 to 1788',.. in D.J. Mulvaney and J. Peter White (eds), *Australians to 1788* (Fairfax, Syme & Weldon Associates, New South Wales, 1987) pp. 389–411.
[114] Frost, 1980, p. xiii.
[115] *Ibid.*, p. xv.
[116] Shaw, A.G.L., '1788–1810', in Crowley, Frank, (ed.), *A New History of Australia* (Heinemann, Melbourne, 1974) p. 6.
[117] Martin, Ged, in Martin, *op. cit.*, p. 184.
[118] The *Lady Penrhyn* and the *Prince of Wales* were both built in 1786 on the Thames, the latter by Christopher Watson & Co. See Bateson, *op. cit.*, p. 80.
[119] King, Jonathon, *The First Fleet: the Convict Voyage that founded Australia, 1787–88* (Macmillan, Australia, 1982) p. 29.
[120] Knight, Roger, National Maritime Museum, Greenwich, personal communication. See also Knight, R.J.B., 'Sandwich, Middleton and Dockyard Appointments', *The Mariner's Mirror*, 57, 2 (1971), pp. 175–192.
[121] Letter from T.W. to the editor, dated Dec. 4 1786, *Gentleman's Magazine*, 56, pp. 1018–19.
[122] Oldham, Wilfred., *The Administration of the System of Transportation of British Convicts 1763–1793* (unpublished Ph.D. thesis, 1933, University of London) pp. 364–65.
[123] Middleton to Nepean, 11 December 1786, CO/201/2, Public Record Office, Kew. Knight, Roger, personal communication.
[124] Frost, 1987 (i), p. 142.
[125] *Ibid.*, p. 45.
[126] *Ibid.*, p. 214.

Chapter 2

[1] MacGregor, David, *Merchant Sailing Ships 1775–1815: Their Design and Construction* (Argus Books, Watford, England, 1980) p. 5.
[2] Sutton, Jean, *Lords of the East: the East India Company and its Ships* (Conway, London, 1981) p. 38.
[3] Dodds, James, and Moore, James, *Building the Wooden Fighting Ship* (Hutchinson, London, 1984) p. 19.
[4] King, Philip Gidley, *The Journal of Philip Gidley King, Lieutenant RN, 1787–1790* Fidlon, P., and Ryan, R. (eds) (Australian Documents Library, Sydney, 1980) p. 5.
[5] *Ibid.*, p.5.
[6] King, *op. cit.*, p. 19.
[7] Barnard Eldershaw, M., *Phillip of Australia* (Angus & Robertson, Sydney, 1938) p. 34.
[8] *Oxford English Dictionary*.
[9] Sutton, *op. cit.*, p. 55. See also Davis, Ralph, *The Rise of the English Shipping Industry* (David and Charles, Newton Abbot, Devon, 1962) p. 417.
[10] Hardy, Horatio, *Register of Ships Employed in the Service of the Hon. East India Company 1760–1812* (1813).
[11] S. S. D. to anonymous, 12 Nov. 1781, Deptford Yard Letter Book, ADM/106/3320, Public Record Office, Kew.
[12] Bateson, Charles, *The Convict Ships, 1787–1868* (Reed, Australian edition, Artarmon, New South Wales, 1974) p. 80.
[13] Knight, R. J. B., *Portsmouth Dockyard Papers 1774–1783. The American War* (City of Portsmouth, Portsmouth, 1987) p. xvii.
[14] Syrett, *op. cit.*, p. 8.
[15] S. S. D. to anonymous, 12 Nov. 1781, Deptford Yard Letter Book, ADM/106/3320, Public Record Office, Kew.
[16] Warrant of 16 Feb. 1781, Deptford Yard Letter Book, ADM/106/3472, Public Record Office, Kew.

REFERENCES 157

[17] Anonymous, 18 Jan. 1782, Deptford Yard Letter Book, ADM/106/3320. Public Record Office, Kew. See also anonymous, 13 Sept. 1781, Deptford Yard Letter Book, ADM/106/3472, Public Record Office, Kew.
[18] Miller, Russell, *The East Indiamen* (Time–Life, Amsterdam, 1980) p. 125.
[19] Chapman, Fredrik, *Architectura Navalis Mercatoria 1768* (Edward Sweetman Co. edition, New York, 1967).
[20] MacGregor, *op. cit.*, p. 172.
[21] Ships Built and Repaired, 1779, ADM/106/3122, Public Record Office, Kew.
[22] S. S. D. to anonymous, 12 Nov. 1781, Deptford Yard Letter Book, ADM/106/3320, Public Record Office, Kew.
[23] Navy Board return, 29 Sept. 1782, ADM/BP/3. Quoted in Knight, *op. cit.*, p.141.
[24] *Berwick* Log, 11 Jan. 1782, ADM/52/1601, Public Record Office, Kew.
[25] Particulars of materials used for coppering ships 1781, 1 Feb. 1782, Deptford Yard Letter Book, ADM/106/3472, Public Record Office, Kew.
[26] Anonymous, 6 Dec. 1781, Deptford Yard Letter Book, ADM/106/3320. Public Record Office, Kew.
[27] Anonymous, 20 Dec. 1781, Deptford Yard Letter Book, ADM/106/3320, Public Record Office, Kew.
[28] S. S. D., to anonymous, 12 Nov. 1781, Deptford Yard Letter Book, ADM/106/3320, Public Record Office, Kew.
[29] Steel's *Royal Navy List, 1782*. See also Colledge, J. J., *Ships of the Royal Navy* (David and Charles, Newton Abbot, Devon, 1969).
[30] Anonymous, 3 Sept. 1781, ADM/106/2508, Public Record Office, Kew.
[31] Ships Built and Repaired, 1779, ADM/106/3122, Public Record Office, Kew.
[32] King, *op. cit.*, p. 19.
[33] Morriss, Roger, *The Royal Dockyards during the Revolutionary and Napoleonic Wars* (Leicester University Press, 1983) p. 22.
[34] Anonymous, 28 Jan. 1782, Deptford Yard Letter Book, ADM/106/3386, Public Record Office, Kew.
[35] Anonymous, 27 Dec. 1781, Deptford Yard Letter Book, ADM/106/3320, Public Record Office, Kew.
[36] Account of expenses, 17 Jan. 1783, Deptford Yard Letter Book, ADM/106/3320, Public Record Office, Kew. Stores brought the figure up to £6152. See Progress Books.
[37] Account of expenses, 17 Jan. 1782, Deptford Yard Letter Book, ADM/106/3320, Public Record Office, Kew.
[38] *Berwick* Log, 25 Jan. 1782, ADM/52/1601, Public Record Office, Kew.
[39] *Berwick* Log, 13 Feb. 1782, ADM/52/1601, Public Record Office, Kew.
[40] Lloyd, Christopher, 'Victualling of the Fleet in the Eighteenth and Nineteenth Centuries', in Watt, J., Freeman, E., and Bynum, W., *Starving Sailors* (National Maritime Museum, Bristol, 1981) p.10.

Chapter 3

[1] Baynton Prideaux, *Berwick* (off Blackwall) 25 Ap. 1782, ADM/106/3472, Public Record Office, Kew.
[2] *Berwick* Log, ADM/52/1601, Public Record Office, Kew.
[3] Navy Board to Yard Officers, 5 Feb. 1780, POR/A/29. National Maritime Museum, Greenwich. Quoted in Knight, *op.cit.*, p. 84.
[4] Knight, *op.cit.*, p. 1vi.
[5] Anonymous, 3 Dec. 1783, Deptford Yard Letter Book, ADM/106/3320, Public Record Office, Kew.
[6] MacGregor, *op.cit.*, p. 57.
[7] Chapelle, Howard, *The Search for Speed under Sail 1700–1855* (Bonanza Books, New York, 1968) p. 25.
[8] Miller, *op.cit.*, p. 125.
[9] *Berwick*, 9 Jan. 1784, Ships' Sailing Qualities, ADM/95/36, Public Record Office, Kew.
[10] Chapelle, *op. cit.*, p. 29. The speed-length ratio is used to compare the technical excellence of ships.

[11] Cook, Captain James, quoted by Naish, George, 'Shipbuilding', in A *History of Technology. Volume VI, 1750–1850* (Clarendon Press, Oxford, 1958) p. 575.
[12] *Ibid.*
[13] King, *op. cit.*, p. 5.
[14] Anonymous, 15 Ap. 1785, Deptford Yard Letter Book, ADM/106/3364, Public Record Office, Kew.
[15] Survey of *Berwick* taken afloat, 4 May 1785, Deptford Yard Letter Book, ADM/106/3364, Public Record Office, Kew.
[16] Anonymous, 7 Dec. 1785, Deptford Yard Letter Book, ADM/106/3364, Public Record Office, Kew.
[17] Contract Ledger, Bills Passed, *Berwick,* Baynton Prideaux, 17 Mar.1786, ADM/112/172, Public Record Office, Kew.

Chapter 4

[1] Anonymous to Navy Board, 23 Aug. 1786, ADM/A/2815, National Maritime Museum, Greenwich.
[2] Anonymous, 6 Sept 1786, Deptford Yard Letter Book, ADM/106/3321, Public Record Office, Kew.
[3] Anonymous, 27 Sept. 1786, Deptford Yard Letter Book, ADM/106/3321, Public Record Office, Kew.
[4] Anonymous to Navy Office, 4 Oct. 1786, Deptford Yard Letter Book, ADM/106/3472, Public Record Office, Kew.
[5] Anonymous, 11 Oct. 1786, Deptford Yard Letter Book, ADM/106/3321, Public Record Office, Kew.
[6] Anonymous to Navy Board, 12 Oct. 1786, ADM/A/2816, National Maritime Museum, Greenwich.
[7] Anonymous, 25 Oct. 1786, Deptford Yard Letter Book, ADM/106/3321, Public Record Office, Kew.
[8] An estimate of expenses, 29 Dec. 1786, ADM/106/2347, Public Record Office, Kew.
[9] This feature sometimes led to theft. See anonymous, 28 Feb.1787, ADM/106/2287, Public Record Office, Kew.
[10] Navy Board to Teer, 3 Jan. 1787, ADM/106/2347, Public Record Office, Kew.
[11] Teer to anonymous, 5 Jan. 1787, ADM/106/2347, Public Record Office, Kew.
[12] Phillip, *Journal,* 5 and 6 Jan. 1787.
[13] Phillip, *Journal,* 22 and 28 Nov. 1786, 1 Dec.1786, 8 Mar.1787.
[14] Anonymous, 10 Oct. 1786, Deptford Yard Letter Book, ADM/106/3321, Public Record Office, Kew.
[15] Anonymous to Navy Board, 12 Oct. 1786, ADM/A/2816, National Maritime Museum, Greenwich.
[16] Anonymous, 25 Oct. 1786, Deptford Yard Letter Book, ADM/106/3321, Public Record Office, Kew.
[17] Anonymous, 31 Oct. 1786., Deptford Yard Letter Book, ADM/106/3321, Public Record Office, Kew.
[18] Teer to Navy Office, 4 Dec. 1786, Deptford Yard Letter Book, ADM/106/3321, Public Record Office, Kew.
[19] An estimate of expenses, 29 Dec. 1786, ADM/106/2347, Public Record Office, Kew
[20] Navy Board to anonymous, 2 Nov. 1786, ADM/G/198, National Maritime Museum, Greenwich.
[21] State and Condition of HMS *Sirius,* 7 Nov. 1786, ADM/106/2214, Public Record Office, Kew.
[22] Phillip, *Journal,* 10 Nov. 1786.
[23] Anonymous to Navy Board, 1 Nov. 1786, ADM/A/2816, National Maritime Museum, Greenwich. See also anonymous, 21 Nov.1786, ADM/106/2214, and anonymous, 11 Dec. 1786, ADM/106/2214, Public Record Office, Kew. Mr Irving's apparatus was fitted to the ship's oven.
[24] Phillip, *Journal,* 24 and 25 Dec. 1786, 28 Jan. 1787.

REFERENCES

[25] Anonymous, 12 Sept. 1786, ADM/106/2796, Public Record Office, Kew.
[26] Anonymous, 12 May 1787, ADM/106/2214, Public Record Office, Kew.
[27] Anonymous to Navy Board, 25 Oct. 1786, ADM/A/2816, National Maritime Museum, Greenwich.
[28] Teer to Navy Office, 4 Dec. 1786, ADM/106/243, Public Record Office, Kew.
[29] Anonymous, 27 Oct. 1786, ADM/36/10978, Public Record Office, Kew.
[30] Anonymous, 7 Nov. 1786, ADM/106/2214, Public Record Office, Kew.
[31] Anonymous, 12 May 1787, ADM/106/2214, Public Record Office, Kew.

Chapter 5

[1] Phillip, Arthur, *Journal*, 31 Jul. 1787. See also George Raper ill. 'Entrance of Rio de Janeiro'.
[2] Some (William Bradley) show four and others (Hunter?) six.
[3] This would be in accordance with a Warrant of 3 Jul. 1786, ADM/106/2509, Public Record Office, Kew.
[4] Eldershaw, *op.cit.*, p. 151. See also King, Jonathan, *The First Fleet* (MacMillan, Melbourne, 1982).
[5] Phillip, *Journal*, 24 Feb. 1787.
[6] Auchmuty, James (ed), *The Voyage of Governor Phillip to Botany Bay* (Sydney, 1970) p.347.
[7] Hunter to anonymous, 24 Feb. 1787, ADM/106/2214, Public Record Office, Kew.
[8] Phillip, *Journal*, 14 Aug. 1787.
[9] Bradley, William, *A Voyage to New South Wales. The Journal of Lieutenant William Bradley RN of HMS Sirius 1786–1792* (Public Library of New South Wales and Ure Smith, 1969) p. 38.
[10] King, Phillip Gidley, *op. cit.*, p.19.
[11] Navy Board to Commissioner Gambier, 24 July 1777, POR/G/1, National Maritime Museum, Greenwich. Quoted in Knight, p.82.
[12] Hunter, Captain John, in Bach, John (ed.), *Captain John Hunter, An Historical Journal 1787–1792* (Angus & Robertson, 1968) p. 61.
[13] Anonymous, 2 Oct. 1781, ADM/106/2508, Public Record Office, Kew.
[14] Eldershaw, *op.cit.*, p. 34.
[15] Clark, Ralph, *Journal*, 22 Nov. 1787, Quoted in King, Jonathan, *op. cit.*, p. 127.
[16] *Ibid.*, p. 124.

Chapter 6

[1] Phillip, Arthur, *Journal*, 10 Ap. 1788.
[2] Hunter, in Bach, *op.cit.*, p. 81.
[3] Anonymous, 18 Oct. 1786, ADM/106/3321, Public Record Office, Kew.
[4] Hunt to anonymous, 4 Sept. 1786, ADM/106/3472, Public Record Office, Kew.
[5] Bradley, *op.cit.*, p. 38.
[6] Hunter, in Bach, *op.cit.*, p. 83.
[7] *Ibid.*, p. 84.
[8] Falconer, William, *Falconer's Marine Dictionary* (1780) (David and Charles Reprint, Newton Abbot, Devon, 1970) p. 243.

Chapter 7

[1] Secretary of the Home Office, quoted in Australian National Parks And Wildlife Service, *Plan of Management, Norfolk Island National Park* (Commonwealth of Australia, 1980) p. 46.
[2] Hunter, in Bach, *op.cit.*, p. 61.
[3] Editor's comment, Bach, *op.cit.*, p. 120.
[4] Clark, Ralph, quoted in Eldershaw, *op.cit.*, p. 327.
[5] Letter from an officer, August 1790, *Historical Records of New SouthWales*, 1: 2, p. 397.
[6] Hunter, in Bach, *op. cit.*, p. 120.
[7] Letter from an officer, Aug. 1790, *Historical Records of New South Wales*, 1: 2 p. 397.
[8] Ross to Phillip, 11 Feb. 1791, *Historical Records of Australia*, 1; p. 231.

160   THE SIRIUS

[9] King, Philip Gidley, in Bach, *op.cit.*, p. 382.
[10] *Ibid*, p. 383.
[11] Hunter, in Bach, *op.cit.*, p.1.

Chapter 8

[1] Masters, P. M. and Flemming, N. C., *Quaternary Coastlines and Marine Archaeology* (Academic Press, London, 1983) p. 622.
[2] MacLeod, Ian, personal communication.
[3] Muckelroy, Keith, *Maritime Archaeology* (Cambridge University Press, Cambridge, 1977) p. 162.
[4] King, Philip Gidley, in Hunter, *An Historical Journal*, p. 241.
[5] Muckelroy, *op cit.*, p. 164.
[6] *Sydney Morning Herald*, 6 Sept 1905, p. 8 and 8 Sept 1905, p. 6.
[7] Anonymous, *Journal of the Proceedings of the Australian Methodists Historical Society*, VI:2 (1938), p. 281.
[8] King, Philip Gidley, in Hunter, *An Historical Journal*, p. 241.
[9] Loney, Jack, *Australian Shipwrecks 1851–1870* (Sydney, 1980) p.205.
[10] Buffet, John, Diary. Norfolk Island. See also Melbourne Register, Australian Shipping Registration Office, Canberra.
[11] Loney, *op. cit.*, p. 26.
[12] Anonymous, 'Raise the Sirius?', *Bicentenary 88*, 2: 3, 1982.
[13] *National Projects and Events* (Australian Bicentennial Authority, February 1983) p. 15.
[14] Henderson, Graeme, 'Report to the Australian Bicentennial Authority on the December 1983 Preliminary Expedition to the Wreck of HMS *Sirius* at Norfolk Island', Western Australian Museum, January 1984, p. 74. Note. The publication of guides such as Kerr, James, *The Conservation Plan* (The National Trust of Australia,1985) now enables the preparation of more explicit conservation plans.
[15] Proudfoot, Helen, 'The First Government House, Sydney', *Heritage Australia*, 2: 2, 1983, p. 21.
[16] Hunter, *Journal* p. 122.
[17] Carpenter, Jon, 'Conservation of a Carronade from the Wrecksite of HMS *Sirius* (1790)', Australian Bicentennial Authority Sirius Project 1986, p. 17.
[18] Frost, Alan, *Convicts and Empire*, p. 218.
[19] Teer to Navy Board, 7 Dec. 1786, ADM/ 106/ 243, 7 Dec. 1786, in Frost, *Arthur Phillip*, p. 146.
[20] Davis, p. 74.

Chapter 9

[1] Tomlin, Maurice, *English Furniture: an Illustrated Handbook* (Faber & Faber, London, 1972) Chapter VIII.
[2] Kerchove, René de, *International Maritime Dictionary* (D. van Nostrand Company, U.S.A., 1948. Second edition 1961) p. 833.
[3] A diameter of 1 ⅛ in is given for keel bolts in Dodds and Moore, *Building the Wooden Fighting Ship*, p. 58
[4] Samuels, L. E., 'The Metallography of Some Copper-Alloy Relics from HMS *Sirius*', *Metallography*, 16: 69–79 (1983) p. 69.
[5] Samuels, *op. cit.*
[6] *Ibid.*, pp. 77–78.
[7] MacLeod, I. D., 'Conservation Report, 1985 Sirius Expedition – Norfolk Island', in Henderson, G., et al., *Report to the Australian Bicentennial Authority on the 1985 Bicentennial Project Expedition to the Wreck of HMS Sirius (1790) at Norfolk Island.* (Report, Department of Maritime Archaeology, Western Australian Maritime Museum, No. 24, 1985) p. 55.
[8] The analysis was done by Ms. Nancy Mills-Reid, formerly of the Department of Materials Conservation, Western Australian Maritime Museum.
[9] Falconer, William, *A New Universal Dictionary of the Marine* (London, 1815. Library Edition, New York. Reprint 1970), p. 561.

[10] Chestnut has good lasting qualities, although for fastenings it does not possess the strength or holding power of other hardwoods. See Kerchove, *op. cit.*, p. 143.
[11] Lavery, Brian, *The Ship of the Line. Volume II: Design, construction and fittings* (Conway Maritime Press, London, 1984) p. 114.
[12] MacLeod, *op. cit.*, pp. 54–55, 59.
[13] A similar spectacle plate was fitted to HMS *Victory*. See Bugler, A., *HMS Victory: Building, restoration and repair* (H.M.S.O., London, 1966) p. 81.
[14] Anonymous, 8 October 1782, Deptford Yard Letter Book, ADM/106/3472, Public Record Office, Kew.
[15] Anonymous, 8 November 1786, ADM/106/3321, Public Record Office, Kew.
[16] Lavery, *op. cit.*, p.121. See also Bugler, *op. cit.*, pp. 78–80.
[17] Examples of cloak pins and/or mirror supports are shown in Gentle, R., and Field, R., *English Domestic Brass 1680 to 1810* (E.P. Dutton, New York, 1975) p. 195.
[18] Similar designs are illustrated in metalwork pattern books in the Victoria and Albert Museum, London: M.63u, accession no. E. 1039–1931, c. 1780-5. See also Goodison, Nicholas, 'The Victoria and Albert Museum's Collection of Metal-Work Pattern Books', *The Journal of the Furniture History Society*, XI (1975), pp. 1–30.
[19] Hunter, John, in Bach, John (ed), *Captain John Hunter, An Historical Journal 1787–1792* (Angus & Robertson, 1968) p. 66.
[20] Brian Lavery, personal. communication.
[21] Warrant No. 441, 3 August 1786, 23 January 1787, ADM/106/2509, Public Record Office, Kew.
[22] Brass fire-grate legs similar to that from the *Sirius* are illustrated in Schiffer, P. *et al.*, *The Brass Book* (Schiffer Publishing, Exton, Pennsylvania, 1978) pp. 262–263.
[23] Examples of engine-turned basaltwares may be seen in Godden, G.A., *British Pottery* (Barrie and Jenkins, London, 1974) pp. 151–173.
[24] Phillip, Arthur, quoted in Frost, *Arthur Phillip*, p. 214.
[25] Anonymous, 11 February 1782, ADM/106/3405, Public Record Office, Kew.
[26] Falconer, *op. cit*, p.30.
[27] The provisions put on board were said to be very good, having been supplied by Zachariah Clarke, the Contractor's Agent who travelled with the First Fleet on board the *Alexander*. See Oldham, Wilfred, *The Administration of the System of Transportation of British Convicts 1763–1793* (unpublished PhD. thesis, 1933, University of London) p. 370.
[28] These are often referred to as 'convict' nails, since the convicts were given the task of making hand-forged nails for use in the colony for building purposes. They are frequently found on land archaeological sites of the early colonial period. Robert Varman, Curator, Norfolk Island, personal communication.
[29] Minutes of the Surveyor's Office, ADM 106/2797, 27 February 1787, Public Record Office, Kew.
[30] Minutes of the Board of Longitude, MRF/L/2 Vol 6 (1), 14 November 1786. National Maritime Museum, Greenwich.
[31] Phillip to the Board of Longitude, 24 November 1786, Records of the Board of Longitude, MRF/L/5 Vol. 12, 121. National Maritime Museum, Greenwich.
[32] Howse, Derek, 'Captain Cook's Marine Timekeepers. Part I - The Kendall Watches', in Howse, Derek and Hutchinson, Beresford, *The Clocks and Watches of Captain James Cook, 1769–1969* (reprinted from the four issues, 1969, of *Antiquarian Horology*, pp. 190–205) p. 192–195.
[33] Howse, *op. cit.*, p. 196.
[34] *Ibid.*, p. 196–197.
[35] Bradley, *op. cit.*, p. 11.
[36] *Ibid.*, pp. 36, 39.
[37] BL 36/301, quoted in Howse, *op. cit.*, p. 197.
[38] Loan of Instruments to Lieut. Dawes 1787–1791. Receipt by A. Phillip, 16 May 1787, Records of the Board of Longitude, MRF/L/5, Vol. 12, 161, National Maritime Museum, Greenwich.
[39] Loan of Instruments to Lieut. Dawes 1787–1791. Receipt by William Dawes, 8 February 1787. Records of the Board of Longitude, MRF/L/5, Vol. 12, 161, National Maritime Museum, Greenwich.

[40] Minutes of the Board of Longitude, MRF/L/2, Vol. 6 (1), 1780-1801, 3 February 1787, National Maritime Museum, Greenwich.

[41] Loan of Instruments to Lieut. Dawes 1787–1791, Receipt dated 8.February Records of the Board of Longitude, MRF/L/5, Vol. 12, 161, National Maritime Museum, Greenwich.

[42] Beresford Hutchinson, Curator, National Maritime Museum, personal communication. It is likely that the watch was taken by Cook on his second and third voyages, and was once owned by Maskelyne. See 'Captain Cook's minor clocks and watches', in Howse and Hutchinson, *op. cit.*, pp. 139–140. See also Britten, F. J., *Old Clocks and Watches and Their Makers* (Batsford, London, 1904) pp. 316–319.

[43] Carpenter, Jon, *et al.*, 'A watch from HMS *Pandora*', *Antiquarian Horology*, 15.6, 1985, pp. 560–601.

[44] Phillip to the Board of Longitude, 18 November 1791, Records of the Board of Longitude, MRF/L/5 Vol. 12, 165, National Maritime Museum, Greenwich.

[45] HMS *Gorgon*, Port Jackson 19 October 1791, Receipt of Instruments. Records of the Board of Longitude, MRF/L/5 Vol. 12,164, National Maritime Museum, Greenwich.

[46] Alan Stimson, National Maritime Museum, personal communication.

[47] Pantographs are referred to in advertisements by John Gilbert, Tycho Brahe and Johnathan Sisson, all famous London instrumentmakers in the eighteenth–century. They may be seen in the collection of eighteenth century trade cards in the Science Museum, London.

[48] Turner, Gerard, L'E., *Antique Scientific Instruments*, (Blandford, Poole, Dorset, 1980) p. 57.

[49] Kimpton, Geoff, 'Construction of an Anchor Stock for the *Sirius* Anchor Displayed at Kingston, Norfolk Island', in Henderson, G., *et al.*, *Australian Bicentennial Authority Project, 1987 Expedition Report on the Wreck of HMS Sirius (1790 at Norfolk Island)*. (Report – Department of Maritime Archaeology, Western Australian Maritime Museum, No. 28, 1987), pp. 62-68.

[50] Falconer, *op. cit.*, p. 12.

[51] *Ibid.*, p. 14.

[51] Falconer, *op. cit.*, p. 14.

[52] Navy Office to Admiralty,12 December 1781, ADM/BP/2, National Maritime Museum, Greenwich.

[53] Carpenter, Jon, *op. cit.*, p.17.

[54] Baker,H. A., 'The Crisis in Naval Ordnance', *National Maritime Museum Maritime Monographs and Reports*, 56 (1983), p. 5.

[55] *Ibid.*

[56] Brian Lavery, personal communication.

[57] *Ibid.*

[58] *Ibid.*

[59] Vaughan Evans, personal communication, and Jeremy Green, *Survey and catalogue of guns in Australia*, (in preparation),Western Australian Maritime Museum.

[60] Graham Wilson, personal communication. See also ML SV8/NORF 1/5.

[61] Governor King to Earl Camden, 30 April 1805, *Historical Records of New South Wales*, 5, p.597.

[62] Wilkinson-Latham, Robert, *British Artillery on Land and Sea 1790–1820*. (David & Charles, Newton Abbot, 1973) p. 30.

[63] *Ibid.*, p. 31.

[64] *Ibid.* p. 31.

[65] *Ibid*, p. 27.

[66] Boxer, E. M., *Diagrams of Guns referred to in Treatise on Artillery, Prepared for use of the Royal Military Academy, Section 2 – Part II* (H.M.S.O., London, 1853)

[67] Bailey, D.W., *British Military Longarms 1715–1865* (Arms and Armour Press, London,1986) p. 30.

[68] M. Murray-Flutter, Assistant Curator, Royal Armouries, personal communication.

[69] Bailey, *op. cit.*, p. 31.

[70] *Ibid*, pp. 12–13.

[71] Moore, John, *The First Fleet Marines 1786–1792*, (University of Queensland Press, St Lucia, 1987) p. 41.

[72] Frost, 1987, p. 156.

[73] M. Murray-Flutter, personal communication.

[74] The size of the musket and pistol shot from the *Sirius* corresponds with shot of ½, ⅝, and ¾ in from the wreck of HMS *Invincible* (1758). See Bingeman, John M., Interim report on artefacts recovered from *Invincible* (1758) between 1979 and 1984 (*International Journal of Nautical Archaeology*, 14, 3 (1985), p. 203).

[75] Musket balls with 'lips' were also recovered from HMS *Invincible*. See Bingeman, *op. cit.*, p. 204.

[76] Held, R., *The Age of Firearms* (Cassell, London, 1957) p. 112.

[77] Montague, Roland H., *Dress and Insignia of the British Army in Australia and New Zealand 1770–1870* (Library of Australian History, Sydney, 1981).

[78] *Ibid.*, p. 18.

[79] Specht, Jim, 'The Early History of Norfolk Island', *Australian Natural History*, 19.7 (1978), p. 223.

[80] Petrological analysis of the stone undertaken by Professor Isabel McBryde of the Department of Prehistory and Anthropology, Australian National University, shows it to be 'spotted pelitic hornfels', a stone which does not outcrop in the coastal Sydney basin but could well be found in the cobbles of the rivers flowing into it from the mountains to the west. As yet the exact source of these outcrops is still to be determined.

[81] A similar stone axe head is illustrated in Arthur Phillip's *The Voyage to Botany Bay*, 1789, p. 137.

[82] Dickson, F. P., *Australian Stone Hatchets* (Academic Press, Australia, 1981) p. 65.

[83] Kelly, David, '*Sirius* Edgeground Hatchet Head Resin Analysis', in Henderson, G. *et al.*, *Australian Bicentennial Authority Project, 1987 Expedition Report on the Wreck of HMS Sirius (1790) at Norfolk Island* (Report – Department of Maritime Archaeology, Western Australian Maritime Museum, No. 28, 1987), p. 61.

[84] Proton and carbon-thirteen nuclear magnetic resonance spectroscopy was carried out by Dr. Emil Ghisalberti of the Organic Chemistry Department, University of Western Australia.

[85] Anonymous, 8 December 1786, ADM/106/2347, Public Record Office, Kew.

[86] Bradley, *op. cit.*, p. 129.

[87] Phillip to anonymous, 1788. ADM 106/2214, Public Record Office, Kew.

Index

Admiralty 18, 28, 33, 38, 58, 59, 60, 110, 148
Adventure 17
Alarm 47
Alexander 33, 68
American-built ships 14
American colonies 8, 12–14, 15, 21, 23, 24, 31
American War of Independence (1776–83) 8, 21, 22–3, 24, 25, 27, 31, 32, 33, 72
ammunition 34, 49, 113, 114, 138–41, *139, 141*, 142–3, 163
anchors 52–3, 63, 95–6, *96, 97, 97*, 100, 106, 107, 130-3
archaeological investigation 89–90
Armed Neutrality of 1780 21
artefacts
    conservation 109, *109, 115, 128*, 146
    control 147–8
    deterioration *91*, 93
    distribution 106–9, 113–45
    identification 111
    preservation 92–3
    recovery 94–6
    registration 146
Astrolabe 101
Atlantic trade 12–3, 14, 15, 18, 36
Australian ICOMOS (International Council on Monuments and Sites) 101
Australian Aborigines 113, 143, 144–5
Australian Bicentennial Authority 7, 100, 101, 103, 109, 110, 146, 147, 148

Ball, Lieutenant Lidgbird 81, 127
ballast 55, 62–3, 106, 107, 108, 111, 113, 123-4, 135, 138
Baltic timber ships 20, 37–8
Baltic trade 17–21, 30, 36, 37–8
Baltic trading ships 39, 40, 112
Batavia 90
Berwick renamed *Sirius* 38, 61
Bird, John 11
Bittern 98
Bligh, Captain William 46
Blomefield, Major General Sir Thomas 137

Blue Fin 99
boats carried on *Sirius* 66, 84
Borrowdale 33, 73
Bounty 46, 88, 101, 112
Bounty Museum 130
Boussole 101
Bradley, Lieutenant William 70, *80, 82*, 86, 106, 144
brassware 113, 114, 117, 121–2, 124, 142, 143
Britannia 52
British navy 16, 22, 23, 29, 36, 51, 58, 76, 153
Brodie's airing stoves 121
Burra Charter 101

Cape Town, *Sirius* voyage to, 1788 74–8, 143
Carron Iron Company 124, 133, 134, 136, 137
carronades *see* guns
Carysfort 61
Catherine, Empress of Russia 21
ceramic ware
    basaltware 113, 123
    porcelain 114, 123
    stoneware 107, 113, 130
Charlotte 33, 73
chronometers 125, 126, *126*
Clark, Lieutenant Ralph 72, 73, 85
Cohen, Barry 147
colonial policy 15–16, 20
colonisation of Australia 28–32
convicts 8, 14, 29, 33, *33*, 34, 66, 74, 79, 85, 88, 107, 145
Cook, Captain James 8, 11, 17, 28, 30, 53, 57, 143
copper fastenings 47, 65, 66, 113, 116–7, *117*, 118, 124
copper sheathing of ships' hulls 17, 18, 36–7, 54, 71, 75–6, 77
    Berwick 47–8
    Sirius 61, 69, 74, 75–7, 119
'country ships' 39
crew 66–8
    armourer 141

boatswain 130
carpenter 72, 74, 75, 78, 133
gunner 133
master 130
officers 67, 120, 121, 143
surgeon 130
see also specific officers' names, e.g. Phillip, Governor Arthur
crime 26

Dawes, Lieutenant William 125, 126
Department of Arts, Heritage and Environment 102, 103
Department of Arts, Sport, the Environment, Tourism and Territories 99
Department of Home Affairs and Environment 99, 100
Deptford Dockyard 23, 38, 39, 40, 41, 46, 47, 50, 54, 57, 58, 59, 66, 71, 77
Diout 98
Discovery 17
Douglas, Charles 50
Drake, Captain, RN 95
dry rot 72
Dutch flyboats 38

East coast colliers 37
'East country' 39
East India Company 22, 27–8
East Indiamen 16, 33, 34, 37, 44, 46, 53, 55–6, 112
 Sirius mistaken for East Indiaman 39–40
Eastern trade 13, 14, 15, 17, 27–8, 29, 30–1, 32, 36, 37
Eastland Company 19
Eglinton 90
Eldershaw, M. Barnard 39, 46, 72
Ellicott, Edward 127
Ellicott, John 127
Endeavour 17, 46, 57, 101, 112
Enlightenment ideas 8

Fairlie 98
Farmer 58
figurehead 58, 69
firearms *see* guns; muskets; ammunition
First Fleet 7, 30, 32, 60, 69–73, 76, 110, 111
First Fleet ships 33–4, 64, 66, 72, 73
Fishburn 34, 68
flax 18, 19, 29, 30
Flora 67
food *see* victuals

Francis 138
Friendship (First Fleet transport) 33, 72
Friendship (schooner wrecked off Norfolk Island, 1835) 98
Frost, Alan 31–2, 111–2
furniture and fittings 120–3

glassware 107, 113, 114, 123, 124, 130
Golden Grove 34
Gorgon 127
guns 49, 49–50, 133–8
 carried by *Berwick* 49
 carried by *Sirius* 63–4, 134–6
 removal for Cape Town voyage 74
 salvaged from *Sirius* 87, 107, 134–6, 138

Hanseatic League 19
Harriet 52
heating of ships 121
hemp 18, 19, 29, 36
Hervey, Augustus 11
Historic Shipwrecks Act (1976) 90, 99, 102, 148
Ho Ho 98
Holmburn 95
Howe, Admiral 61
Hunter, Lieutenant-Governor John 74, 75, 77, 79, 81, 83, 86, 88, 106, 107, 125, 144

Induna 95
Iris 98
iron industry 18, 24

James Matthews 90

Kentledge 62
 see also ballast
King, Philip Gidley 38–9, 50, 57, 71, 73, 79, 94, 97
Kingston (Norfolk Island) 79, 84, 99

Lady Penrhyn, 33, 73, 156
Langlois, Claude 129
Larcum Kendall's Marine Timekeeper K1 125, 126, *126*, 127
Lively 90
livestock 85
logbooks 111
London (England) 12
Lord Howe Island 74

maritime archaeology 90–2
 and history 89–90, 112, 148
Marquis Cornwallis 138

Mary Hamilton 98, 99, 108
Mary Ogilvie 98
Maskelyne, Dr Nevil 125, 126, 127
Mason, John 40
masts
    Sirius' 41, 48, 55, 59, 69, 107
    timber for 18, 19, 20, 30, 36
Matai 99
Mather, James 40
Matra, James 30–1
Mayflower 40
Middleton, Charles 34
Minerva 52
Muckelroy, Keith
    study of the wreck sites 93–4, 101, 111
Museums Association of Australia 110
muskets 107, 114, 141–2, *145*

nautical instruments 113, 114, 125–30
navigation *see* nautical instruments
Navy Board 22, 33, 39, 41, 59, 61, 71
New Holland 28–9
New South Wales, decision to settle 28–32
New Zealand flax plant 29–30
Norfolk 98
Norfolk Island 79, 88, 138
    discovery and settlement 30, 32, 138
    loss of *Sirius* off 7, 81–5
Norfolk Islanders 95, 98, 100, 102, 107, 109, 146, 147, 148
North American colonies *see* American colonies

ordnance *see* guns; muskets; ammunition

Pandora 65, 76, 90, 101, 119, 120, 124, 127
pantographs 129–30, *131*, 162
patronage system 10
Penang, annexation by Britain (1786) 31
Phillip, Governor Arthur 7, 11, 34–5, 38, 62, 63, 64, 66, 67, 70, 71, 72, 77, 79, 85, 86, 123, 125, 126, 127, 144
Pitcairn Islanders 88
Pitt, William, the Younger 24–5, 26–7, 28, 29, 31
Port Jackson, settlement at 74
poverty 9, 26
Prideaux, Lieutenant Baynton 52, 54, 55, 56, 58
Prince of Wales 33, 40, 156
pump systems 17, 75, 119–20, 133
Punch, Gary 148

Ramsden, Jesse 11, 126, 127, 128, 129
Rangi 99
Raper, George 76, 83
Rapid 90
relics of *Sirius* 113–45
    fire grate leg 113–4, *122*
    pantograph 129–30, *131*
    relating to crew and passengers 125–45
    sextant 128–9, *128*
    shoulder-belt plates 6, 114, 143
    spectacle plate 53, 108, 118–9, 161
    stone hatchet 113, 143–5, *163*
    structure and fittings 116–24
    see also ammunition; anchors; artefacts; brassware; ceramic ware; copper fastenings; glassware; guns
Renaki 98, 107
Resolution 17, 46, 101, 112
rigging 124, 130
Ross, Lieutenant-Governor Robert 87
Rotherhithe shipyard 7, *37*, 40, 58
Rousseau, Jean-Jacques 24
Royal Marines 67, 114, 143
Royal Naval Academy 125
Royal Navy *see* British navy
rudder 108, 118–9

sails 48, 56–7, 87, 130
Scarborough 33
Scheiner, Christoph 129
scurvy 74, 130
Seven Years War (1756–63) 21
sextants 127–9, *128*
shipbuilding 14, 17–21, 36–8, 40, 112
    refitting 54–5
    job system, 51
shipping 13, 16–7
shipwrecks 90–2
    off Norfolk Island 97–9
Shortland, Lieutenant John 33
Sirius, name change from *Berwick* 38, 61
Sirius Project 7, 99ff., 146–8
    1983 expedition 100
    strategy 102
    1985 expedition 103–9
    1987 expedition 109–10, 146, 147
    1987 archival investigation 110–1
    1988 expedition 147–8
Sirius wreck site 90–1, 94, 101–2, *103*, *104*, *105*, 106–9, 110
slave trade 13, 14, 25

social class and mobility 9–11
South Australian Department of Environment and Planning 110
Spode porcelain 123
Stella Maris 97
stores 65, 116
stoves 121–2
Supply 33, 50, 64, 72, 73, 74, 76, 77, 79, 81, 97, 112, 127
Suttor, Sir Francis 94–5
Sydney Cove 90
Sydney, Lord 29, 59, 70

Tasmanian National Parks and Wildlife Service 103
Teer, Captain George 34, 62, 63, 64, 67, 112
timber supplies 18, 19
Treaty of Versailles (1783) 57–8

unemployment 25–6, 153
United States of America 28, 54

Venerable 83
Vergulde Draeck 90

Victoria Archaeological Survey 103
victuals 53, 58, 65, 77, 87, 124, 130, 161
war and trade 21–2
War of the Spanish Succession (1701–13) 21
Warrigal 98
water supply 65, 66, 124, 130
Watson, Christopher, & Co 40, 58
Wedgewood, Josiah 113, 123, 153
West Indies 13, 14, 16–7, 22, 23
    possible voyage of *Berwick* to 57
Western Australian Maritime Museum 92, 110, 132
Western Australian Museum 96, 100, 103, 109
    survey of wreck sites 90
White, Surgeon John 144
Wilberforce, William 25

Young, Sir George 30

Zeewijk 90
Zuytdorp 90

Acknowledgments

The authors wish to thank the following organisations for their involvement in the *Sirius* Project: the Australian Bicentennial Authority, Avon Inflatable, British Airways, East-West Airlines, Ipec, the Museums Association of Australia (NSW Branch), the National Maritime Museum at Greenwich in England, the Norfolk Island Administration Works Depot, the Norfolk Island Government, Norfolk Island Hospital, the Public Record Office at Kew in England, the South Australian Department of Environment and Planning, the Tasmanian Parks and Wildlife Service, the Victoria Archaeological Survey, the Western Australian Department of Land Administration (Cartographic Services Branch) and the Western Australian Museum.

We are also indebted to the following individuals for their assistance with the project and with the production of this book: Byron Adams, Ross Allomes, Jennifer Amess, Puss Anderson, Terry Arnott, Karen Atkinson, Patrick Baker, John Bannister, The Hon. Geoff Bennett, Bill Blucher, Frank Broeze, Les Brown, Paul Brown, The Hon. David Buffett, Byron Burrell, Jon Carpenter, Barley Christian, Garry Christian, Margaret Christian, Paul Clark, The Hon. Barry Cohen, Kerry Coop, Sue Cox, Peter Currie, Karl Davies, Richard Douran, Gordon Duval, Maree Edmiston, Jan Edwards, Peter Ely, Borry Evans, Morgan Evans, Vaughan Evans, Dena Garrett, Emil Ghisalberti, Mollie Gillen, Jeremy Green, Gill, Mavis and Karlene Hitch, Merval Hoare, Beresford Hutchinson, Ken Jackson, Bill Jeffery, Mike Johnston, David Kelly, Ian Kenny, Geoff Kimpton, Helen Kimpton, Roger Knight, Alfred Knightbridge, Brian Lavery, John Lawking, Eric van Leeuwen, Tom van Leeuwen, Tim and Tom Lloyd, David Lyon, Isabel McBryde, Mike McCarthy, Bev McCoy, Lindsay McFarlane, Ian McLeod, Commodore and Mrs J. A. Matthew, Sally May, David Millar, Nancy Mills-Reid, Roger Morriss, Ray Mulligan, M. Murray-Flutter, John Nobbs, Steve Nobbs, Rena Prentice, Eric Powell, The Hon. Gary Punch, Franklin Randall, Steve Richards, Kevin Robinson, Michael Roper, Ted and Jan Semple, Mike Simpson, John M. Smith, Mary Smith, Mark Staniforth, Rick Swansborough, Alan Stimson, Neil and Judy Tavener, Jim Tavener, Christina Tophan, Bob Towns, Sharon Towns, Air Vice Marshal Ken Trebilco, Robert Varman, Alec Wagstaff, Alex Werner, Bob White, Graham Wilson, Jon Womersley and the people of Norfolk Island.